SAN SEBASTIAN TRAVEL GUIDE 2024

Your Ultimate Guide to Beaches, Cuisine, Culture, and Adventures in the Basque Jewel"

ROBSON PHILLIP

All rights reserved. No part of this publication may be reproduced, distributed, or transmitted in any form or by any means, including photocopying, recording, or other electronic or mechanical methods, without the prior written permission of the publisher, except in the case of brief quotations embodied in critical reviews and certain other noncommercial uses permitted by copyright law.

Copyright © Robson Phillip, 2024.

Table of Contents

Introduction 8
    Welcome to San Sebastian 8
    How to Use This Guide 10
    Overview of San Sebastian 15

Getting There 18
    By Air 18
    By Train 20
    By Bus 21
    By Car 23

Getting Around 27
    Public Transportation 27
    Trains 29
    Funicular 30
    Taxis and Ridesharing 31
    Biking 33
    Walking Tours 36
    Guided Walking Tours 37
    Hiking Trails 39

Accomodation 41
    Luxury Hotels 42
    Budget Accommodation 47
    Hostels 50

Airbnb and Vacation Rentals 52

Vacation Rentals 54

Neighborhoods And Districts 56

Parte Vieja (Old Town) 57

Gros 59

Antiguo 61

Centro 63

Amara 65

Top Attractions 69

La Concha Beach 70

Monte Urgull 72

San Telmo Museum 74

Kursaal Congress Centre 76

Aquarium San Sebastian 79

Cultural Experiences 83

Basque Culture and Traditions 84

Local Festivals and Events 86

Art Galleries and Museums 89

Music and Performing Arts 92

Outdoor Activities 96

Beaches and Water Sports 97

Hiking and Nature Walks 100

Cycling Routes 103

Parks and Gardens 105

- Culinary Delights 110
  - Pintxos Bars 111
  - Traditional Basque Cuisine 113
  - Top Michelin-Starred Restaurants 116
  - Food Markets and Culinary Tours 118
- Nightlife and Entertainment 123
  - Bars and Pubs 124
  - Nightclubs 126
  - Live Music Venues 128
  - Theaters and Cinemas 131
- Shopping 136
  - Local Markets 137
  - Boutique Stores 140
  - Shopping Malls 143
  - Souvenirs and Artisan Goods 146
- Day Trips from San Sebastian 152
  - Getaria 153
  - Hondarribia 155
  - Zarautz 158
  - Biarritz (France) 160
- Practical Information 164
  - Emergency Contacts 165
  - Health and Safety Tips 166
  - Language and Communication 168

Money and Banking 169
Internet and Mobile Connectivity 171
Travel Tips 174
Best Time to Visit 175
Cultural Etiquette 177
Packing Essentials 179
Accessibility Information 181
Conclusion 184
Final Thoughts 184
FAQs 188

Introduction

Welcome to San Sebastian

Nestled along the stunning coastline of northern Spain, San Sebastian, or Donostia as it is known in the Basque language, is a city that captivates visitors with its breathtaking beauty, rich cultural heritage, and culinary excellence. Whether you're a first-time visitor or returning to explore more,

San Sebastian offers a unique blend of tradition and modernity that will leave you enchanted.

Renowned for its picturesque beaches, vibrant cultural scene, and world-class dining, San Sebastian is a destination that caters to a diverse array of interests. From sunbathing on the golden sands of La Concha Beach to hiking up Monte Urgull for panoramic views of the city and its surroundings, there's something for everyone. The city's old town, Parte Vieja, invites you to wander through its narrow streets, discover historic sites, and indulge in the local tradition of pintxos—small, delectable snacks that are a culinary delight.

San Sebastian is more than just a feast for the eyes and taste buds; it's a city where history and culture are deeply ingrained in everyday life. Festivals such as the San Sebastian International Film Festival and the Semana Grande celebrate the city's vibrant spirit and bring people together from all corners of the globe.

In this travel guide, we'll take you on a journey through San Sebastian's many wonders, providing you with all the information you need to make the most of your visit. Whether you're here for a weekend getaway or a longer stay, this guide will help you navigate the city, discover hidden gems, and experience San Sebastian like a local.

How to Use This Guide

This travel guide is designed to be your comprehensive companion as you explore San Sebastian. We've organized the content into sections that cover all aspects of your trip, from practical information to detailed descriptions of attractions and activities. Here's how you can make the most of this guide:

1. **Plan Your Arrival**: The "Getting There" section provides detailed information on how to reach San Sebastian, whether you're flying in, taking a train, or driving. It includes tips on

navigating the city's transport system and advice on the best travel routes.

2. **Navigate the City**: In "Getting Around," you'll find everything you need to know about public transportation, biking, walking tours, and other means of getting around the city. This section will help you move efficiently from one place to another, ensuring you don't miss any must-see locations.

3. **Choose Your Accommodation**: The "Accommodation" section offers a range of options to suit different budgets and preferences, from luxury hotels to budget-friendly hostels. Each option includes descriptions, amenities, and insider tips to help you make an informed choice.

4. **Explore Neighborhoods**: San Sebastian is a city of diverse neighborhoods, each with its own charm. The "Neighborhoods and Districts" section gives you an overview of the main areas,

highlighting key attractions, dining spots, and local experiences.

5. **Discover Top Attractions**: "Top Attractions" is your guide to the city's must-visit sites, from iconic landmarks like La Concha Beach and Monte Urgull to cultural treasures like the San Telmo Museum. Each entry provides historical context, visitor information, and tips to enhance your experience.

6. **Immerse in Culture**: In "Cultural Experiences," you'll learn about the rich Basque culture, local festivals, and the thriving arts scene. This section includes recommendations for galleries, museums, and cultural events that offer a deeper understanding of San Sebastian's heritage.

7. **Enjoy Outdoor Activities**: If you love the outdoors, the "Outdoor Activities" section is for you. It covers everything from beach activities

and water sports to hiking trails and parks, ensuring you can enjoy the natural beauty of San Sebastian.

8. **Savor Culinary Delights**: San Sebastian is a culinary paradise. The "Culinary Delights" section guides you through the city's renowned food scene, including the best pintxos bars, traditional Basque restaurants, and Michelin-starred dining experiences.

9. **Experience Nightlife and Entertainment**: "Nightlife and Entertainment" provides insights into the city's vibrant after-dark scene, from cozy bars and lively nightclubs to live music venues and theaters.

10. **Shop Till You Drop**: For those who love to shop, the "Shopping" section highlights local markets, boutique stores, and shopping malls, offering a range of options for souvenirs and unique finds.

11. **Take Day Trips**: The "Day Trips from San Sebastian" section suggests nearby destinations worth exploring, such as Getaria and Biarritz, providing a perfect break from the city's hustle and bustle.

12. **Practical Information**: To ensure a smooth trip, the "Practical Information" section includes essential details like emergency contacts, health and safety tips, language and communication advice, and money and banking information.

13. **Travel Tips**: In "Travel Tips," you'll find advice on the best times to visit, cultural etiquette, packing essentials, and accessibility information to help you prepare for your journey.

Overview of San Sebastian

San Sebastian, located in Spain's Basque Country, is a coastal city known for its unique blend of natural beauty, cultural richness, and gastronomic excellence. Here are some key highlights:

- **Geography**: San Sebastian is situated along the Bay of Biscay, surrounded by lush hills and the picturesque La Concha Bay. The city's beaches—La Concha, Ondarreta, and Zurriola—are some of the most beautiful in Europe, offering a mix of relaxation and water activities.

- **History**: Founded in the 12th century, San Sebastian has a rich history that is reflected in its architecture, from the historic Parte Vieja to the elegant 19th-century buildings. The city has a storied past, having been a strategic military location and later a summer retreat for Spanish royalty.

- **Culture**: The Basque culture is deeply embedded in the city's identity. This is evident in the local language (Euskara), traditional music and dance, and the many cultural festivals celebrated throughout the year. The San Sebastian International Film Festival is one of the most prestigious in the world, attracting film enthusiasts and celebrities alike.

- **Culinary Scene**: San Sebastian is often hailed as one of the world's top culinary destinations. The city boasts a high concentration of Michelin-starred restaurants and is famous for its pintxos—bite-sized delights that are a staple of Basque cuisine. The blend of traditional and innovative cooking makes dining here a memorable experience.

- **Outdoor Activities**: The city's natural surroundings offer numerous outdoor activities. You can hike up Monte Igueldo or Monte Urgull for stunning views, enjoy water sports at Zurriola Beach, or take a leisurely stroll along the scenic Paseo Nuevo.

- **Events and Festivals**: San Sebastian hosts a variety of events throughout the year, including the Tamborrada (Drum Festival), Semana Grande (Big Week), and numerous regattas. These events showcase the city's lively spirit and provide a unique insight into local traditions.

San Sebastian is a city that invites exploration and promises to leave a lasting impression. Whether you're here to relax on the beach, delve into history, indulge in world-class cuisine, or experience the vibrant culture, San Sebastian offers something for everyone. This guide will help you uncover the best the city has to offer and ensure that your visit is both enjoyable and unforgettable.

Getting There

San Sebastian, with its stunning coastal scenery and rich cultural heritage, is easily accessible by various modes of transportation. Whether you prefer flying, taking a train, traveling by bus, or driving, there are convenient options to suit your needs. In this section, we'll provide detailed information on how to reach San Sebastian, ensuring a smooth and enjoyable journey.

By Air

San Sebastian is serviced by several nearby airports, making air travel a convenient option for many visitors.

San Sebastian Airport (EAS)

Located just 20 kilometers from the city center, San Sebastian Airport is the closest airport to the city. It offers limited domestic and international flights, primarily connecting with Madrid and Barcelona. From the airport, you can reach the city center by taxi, which takes approximately 20 minutes, or by taking a bus, which offers a more budget-friendly option.

Bilbao Airport (BIO)

Bilbao Airport, situated about 100 kilometers west of San Sebastian, is the largest and most well-connected airport in the region. It serves numerous international and domestic flights, making it a popular choice for travelers. To reach San Sebastian from Bilbao Airport, you can take a direct bus, which operates frequently and takes around 75 minutes. Alternatively, you can rent a car and drive, which offers the flexibility to explore the surrounding Basque Country.

Biarritz Airport (BIQ)

Located 50 kilometers north of San Sebastian, Biarritz Airport in France is another viable option for international travelers. It offers flights from major European cities and seasonal connections from further afield. From Biarritz Airport, you can reach San Sebastian by taking a bus or train, both of which offer scenic routes along the coastline and take approximately an hour.

By Train

Traveling by train to San Sebastian is a comfortable and scenic option, with several rail services connecting the city to major destinations in Spain and France.

RENFE (Spanish National Railways)

San Sebastian is well-connected to the Spanish rail network through RENFE, with the primary train station being Estación del Norte. High-speed trains (Alvia and AVE) provide direct and indirect services from major Spanish cities such as Madrid, Barcelona, and Zaragoza. The journey from Madrid to San Sebastian takes around 5 hours, while the trip from Barcelona takes approximately 6 hours. Train travel offers the advantage of comfortable seating, scenic views, and the opportunity to relax as you approach the city.

SNCF (French National Railways)

For those traveling from France, SNCF provides convenient connections to San Sebastian. The TGV high-speed train from Paris to Hendaye, a town on the French-Spanish border, takes around 4.5 hours. From Hendaye, you can take the Euskotren, a local train service that runs frequently to San Sebastian, with a journey time of just over 30 minutes. This option allows you to enjoy the scenic beauty of both French and Spanish Basque Country.

By Bus

Bus travel is a cost-effective and efficient way to reach San Sebastian, with numerous services connecting the city to various destinations in Spain and beyond.

ALSA

ALSA, Spain's leading bus company, operates extensive routes to San Sebastian from major cities such as Madrid, Barcelona, Bilbao, and Pamplona. Buses are equipped with comfortable seating, Wi-Fi, and onboard entertainment, ensuring a pleasant journey. The trip from Madrid takes around 6 hours, while the journey from Barcelona takes approximately 7.5 hours. ALSA also offers international routes from cities like Paris and Lisbon, making it a convenient option for travelers from abroad.

PESA

PESA is another prominent bus company serving the Basque region. It offers frequent services from nearby cities such as Bilbao and Vitoria-Gasteiz, with journey times of around 1.5 to 2 hours. PESA buses are known for their punctuality and comfort, providing a reliable option for regional travel.

Eurolines

For international travelers, Eurolines operates long-distance bus services connecting San Sebastian with major European cities. This includes routes from Paris, Bordeaux, and Brussels. While bus travel may take longer than other modes of transportation, it offers an affordable way to reach San Sebastian and the opportunity to enjoy the landscapes along the way.

By Car

Driving to San Sebastian provides the flexibility to explore the region at your own pace and enjoy the scenic beauty of the Basque Country.

From Spain

If you're driving from within Spain, several highways connect San Sebastian to major cities.

The A-1 and AP-1 highways link Madrid to San Sebastian, with a journey time of approximately 4.5 to 5 hours. From Barcelona, you can take the AP-2 and AP-68 highways, which take around 6 hours. The AP-8 highway connects Bilbao to San Sebastian, with a drive time of about 1 hour. These routes offer well-maintained roads and the chance to take detours to explore charming towns and landscapes along the way.

From France

For those driving from France, the A63 and AP-8 highways provide a direct route from Bordeaux to San Sebastian, with a journey time of around 2.5 hours. From Biarritz, it's a quick 45-minute drive along the N-10 and AP-8 highways. The French and Spanish road networks are well-integrated, making cross-border travel smooth and straightforward.

Parking and Navigation

San Sebastian offers various parking options, including public parking garages and on-street parking. The city center can be challenging to navigate due to narrow streets and pedestrian zones, so it's advisable to park in designated areas and explore the city on foot or using public transportation. Some recommended parking facilities include Parking La Concha, Parking Kursaal, and Parking Buen Pastor, all of which are centrally located and provide easy access to major attractions.

Car Rentals

If you prefer the convenience of having a car during your stay, numerous car rental agencies operate in San Sebastian, including international brands such as Avis, Hertz, and Europcar, as well as local companies. Renting a car allows you to explore the surrounding Basque Country, including picturesque coastal towns, rolling hills, and scenic countryside.

You can choose to fly, take a train, travel by bus, or drive, reaching San Sebastian is straightforward and offers various options to suit your preferences and budget. Each mode of transportation has its own advantages, from the speed and convenience of air travel to the scenic routes of train and bus journeys, and the flexibility of driving. Once you arrive, you'll find San Sebastian to be a welcoming and accessible city, ready to charm you with its beauty, culture, and culinary delights.

Getting Around

San Sebastian is a compact and walkable city with a well-developed transportation system that makes it easy to navigate. Whether you prefer public transportation, taxis, ridesharing, biking, or walking, there are plenty of options to help you get around and explore all that this beautiful city has to offer.

Public Transportation

San Sebastian's public transportation system is efficient, reliable, and affordable, making it an excellent choice for getting around the city.

Buses

San Sebastian's bus network is extensive, covering the entire city and its surrounding areas. The bus service is operated by Dbus, the local public transport company, which runs over 30 routes.

- **Main Routes**: Key routes include Line 5 (connecting the Old Town with Gros and Amara), Line 13 (linking Antiguo with the city center), and Line 16 (providing access to the Ondarreta and La Concha beaches). The buses are frequent, with most routes operating every 10-15 minutes during peak hours.

- **Night Buses**: For late-night travelers, Dbus operates several night bus routes (known as "Búhos") on weekends and holidays. These buses run from around midnight until the early hours of the morning, ensuring you have a safe way to return to your accommodation after a night out.

- **Fares**: A single bus ticket costs around €1.75. You can purchase tickets directly from the driver or use a contactless travel card, the Mugi card, which offers discounted fares and can be topped up at various locations around the city.

- **Accessibility**: Buses in San Sebastian are equipped with ramps and designated spaces for wheelchair users, making them accessible for all travelers.

Trains

While San Sebastian is well-served by buses, the city also has a suburban train service operated by Euskotren, connecting San Sebastian with nearby towns and cities.

- **Routes**: The primary route is the E2 line, which runs from Hendaye (France) to Lasarte-Oria, passing through key stops such as Gros, Amara, and Anoeta. The train is an excellent option for day trips to nearby destinations like Zarautz and Getaria.

- **Fares**: Ticket prices vary depending on the distance traveled, with a journey from San Sebastian to Zarautz costing around €2.50.

Tickets can be purchased at stations or using the Mugi card.

- **Frequency**: Trains run every 15-30 minutes, depending on the time of day and the specific route.

Funicular

San Sebastian's funicular railway offers a unique and scenic way to travel between the city and the top of Monte Igueldo.

- **Route**: The funicular departs from the lower station near Ondarreta Beach and ascends to the amusement park at the summit of Monte Igueldo, offering panoramic views of the city and the Bay of Biscay.

- **Fares**: A round-trip ticket costs around €3.75 for adults and €2.50 for children. Tickets can be purchased at the funicular station.

- **Frequency**: The funicular operates every 15 minutes during peak season (summer) and less frequently during the off-season.

Taxis and Ridesharing

For those who prefer the convenience of door-to-door service, taxis and ridesharing options are readily available in San Sebastian.

Taxis

Taxis are a reliable and efficient way to get around San Sebastian, especially for short trips or when carrying luggage.

- **Availability**: Taxis can be found at designated ranks throughout the city, including at major transportation hubs such as the train station and the airport. You can also hail a taxi on the street or book one by phone.
- **Fares**: Taxi fares are metered, with a base fare of around €3.50 and an additional charge of

approximately €1.10 per kilometer. There may be extra charges for luggage, late-night trips, and travel on public holidays.

- **Accessibility**: Some taxis are equipped with facilities for wheelchair users. It's advisable to request an accessible taxi when booking to ensure availability.

Ridesharing

Ridesharing services like Uber and Cabify operate in San Sebastian, offering an alternative to traditional taxis.

- **Booking**: Rides can be booked via mobile apps, providing the convenience of cashless payments and real-time tracking of your ride.

- **Fares**: Ridesharing fares are generally competitive with taxi fares and may vary depending on demand and distance.

- **Service Quality**: Ridesharing vehicles are typically newer and offer a comfortable and clean travel experience.

Biking

San Sebastian is a bike-friendly city with an extensive network of cycling paths and a public bike-sharing system, making it easy to explore the city on two wheels.

Cycling Paths

San Sebastian boasts over 30 kilometers of dedicated cycling paths, known as "bidegorris," which connect key areas of the city and provide a safe and scenic way to travel.

- **Key Routes**: Popular cycling routes include the path along La Concha Bay, which offers stunning views of the beach and the sea, and the route from the city center to the neighborhoods of Gros and Antiguo. The paths are well-marked and maintained, ensuring a pleasant ride.

- **Safety**: Cycling in San Sebastian is generally safe, with most paths separated from motor vehicle traffic. However, it's essential to follow local traffic rules and wear a helmet for added safety.

Public Bike Sharing

San Sebastian's public bike-sharing system, Dbizi, offers a convenient and affordable way to rent bikes for short trips around the city.

- **Stations**: There are over 30 Dbizi stations located throughout San Sebastian, including near major attractions, transportation hubs, and residential areas. Bikes can be rented from and returned to any station.

- **Membership**: To use Dbizi, you need to register online or at a Dbizi station. Membership options include daily, weekly, and annual passes, with prices starting at around €5 for a day pass.

- **Usage**: Once registered, you can rent a bike by scanning your membership card or using the Dbizi mobile app. The first 30 minutes of each ride are usually free, with additional charges for longer rides.

Bike Rentals

In addition to Dbizi, several private companies offer bike rentals, providing a range of options from standard bicycles to electric bikes and tandem bikes.

- **Shops**: Bike rental shops can be found throughout the city, particularly in tourist areas such as the Old Town and along the beachfront. Some popular rental companies include La Bicicleta and Donostibike.

- **Rates**: Rental prices vary depending on the type of bike and the rental duration, with standard bikes starting at around €10 per day. Electric bikes are more expensive but offer the advantage of effortless travel, especially on hilly terrain.

Walking Tours

San Sebastian's compact size and pedestrian-friendly layout make walking one of the best ways to explore the city. Numerous walking tours are available, offering guided experiences that highlight the city's history, culture, and culinary delights.

Self-Guided Walking Tours

For independent travelers, self-guided walking tours allow you to explore San Sebastian at your own pace.

- **Routes**: Popular self-guided routes include the promenade along La Concha Bay, a stroll through the historic Parte Vieja (Old Town), and a hike up Monte Urgull for panoramic views. Detailed maps and itineraries can be found online or at local tourist information centers.

- **Highlights**: Key attractions along these routes include the San Telmo Museum, the iconic Peine del Viento sculptures, the bustling Mercado de la Bretxa, and the scenic Paseo Nuevo.

Guided Walking Tours

For a more in-depth exploration, consider joining a guided walking tour led by knowledgeable local guides.

- **Historical Tours**: Discover San Sebastian's rich history with tours that take you through the city's most significant landmarks, such as the 19th-century Ayuntamiento (City Hall), the

Gothic-style San Vicente Church, and the picturesque Plaza de la Constitución.

- **Culinary Tours**: Experience San Sebastian's world-renowned culinary scene with a pintxos tour, where you'll sample a variety of these delicious Basque tapas at local bars and learn about the city's gastronomic traditions. Some popular companies offering these tours include Devour Tours and Mimo Bite the Experience.

- **Cultural Tours**: Immerse yourself in Basque culture with tours that highlight local traditions, festivals, and the unique Basque language. These tours often include visits to cultural institutions like the Basque Culinary Center and participation in traditional activities such as cider tasting.

Hiking Trails

For those who enjoy nature and outdoor activities, San Sebastian offers several hiking trails that provide breathtaking views of the city and its surroundings.

- **Monte Urgull**: This historic hill offers several trails leading to the summit, where you'll find the Castillo de la Mota and the Sagrado Corazón statue. The trails are well-maintained and suitable for all fitness levels, with plenty of benches and viewpoints along the way.

- **Monte Igueldo**: For a more challenging hike, take the trail up Monte Igueldo, which offers spectacular views of La Concha Bay and the Cantabrian Sea. The trail can be steep in sections, so be sure to wear appropriate footwear and bring water.

- **Paseo de Ulia**: This coastal trail runs from the Gros neighborhood to the nearby town of

Pasaia, offering stunning sea views and the opportunity to explore hidden coves and natural landscapes. The trail is moderately difficult and takes around 3-4 hours to complete.

San Sebastian's diverse and well-developed transportation options make it easy to explore this vibrant city. Whether you prefer the convenience of public transportation, the flexibility of taxis and ridesharing, the freedom of biking, or the immersive experience of walking tours, there's a mode of travel to suit your preferences. With its compact size and pedestrian-friendly layout, San Sebastian invites you to discover its beauty, culture, and culinary delights at your own pace.

Accomodation

San Sebastian offers a diverse range of accommodation options to suit every budget and preference. Whether you're looking for luxury hotels, mid-range establishments, budget accommodations, hostels, or vacation rentals, you'll find plenty of choices to make your stay comfortable and memorable.

Luxury Hotels

San Sebastian is home to several world-class luxury hotels that provide exceptional service, elegant accommodations, and prime locations. Here are some top choices for those seeking a luxurious experience:

Hotel Maria Cristina

Located in the heart of San Sebastian, Hotel Maria Cristina is an iconic luxury hotel that has hosted numerous celebrities and dignitaries since it opened in 1912. The hotel boasts opulent decor, spacious rooms, and a prime location overlooking the Urumea River.

- **Amenities**: Guests can enjoy fine dining at the hotel's restaurant, a well-equipped fitness center, and a full-service spa. The rooms feature plush furnishings, marble bathrooms, and stunning views of the city or river.

- **Special Features**: The hotel offers personalized concierge services, ensuring that guests have access to the best experiences San Sebastian has to offer.

Hotel de Londres y de Inglaterra

With its prime location on La Concha Beach, Hotel de Londres y de Inglaterra offers luxurious beachfront accommodations with spectacular sea views. The hotel combines historic charm with modern amenities.

- **Amenities**: The hotel features a beachfront restaurant, a stylish bar, and elegantly appointed rooms with modern conveniences. Guests can also enjoy direct access to the beach.

- **Special Features**: Many rooms have private balconies with panoramic views of the bay, making it a perfect choice for those who want to wake up to the sound of the waves.

Akelarre Hotel

For a more secluded and exclusive experience, Akelarre Hotel, located on Monte Igueldo, offers luxurious accommodations with breathtaking views of the Cantabrian Sea. This boutique hotel is part of the renowned Akelarre restaurant, which holds three Michelin stars.

- **Amenities**: The hotel offers spacious suites, an infinity pool, a wellness center, and exceptional dining experiences at the Akelarre restaurant. Each suite features contemporary design, private terraces, and sea views.

- **Special Features**: Guests can indulge in gourmet dining experiences and personalized services, including private tours and culinary workshops.

Mid-Range Hotels

San Sebastian offers a variety of mid-range hotels that provide comfortable accommodations and excellent value for money. These hotels are ideal for travelers seeking quality without the luxury price tag.

Hotel Niza

Hotel Niza is a charming mid-range hotel located on La Concha Beach, offering comfortable rooms with stunning sea views. The hotel's Art Deco design and friendly atmosphere make it a popular choice for visitors.

- **Amenities**: The hotel features a beachfront restaurant, free Wi-Fi, and comfortable rooms with modern amenities. Guests can enjoy easy access to the beach and nearby attractions.

- **Special Features**: The hotel's prime location and cozy ambiance make it a great choice for those looking to stay by the sea without breaking the bank.

Hotel Villa Soro

Situated in a beautifully restored 19th-century villa, Hotel Villa Soro offers elegant accommodations in a tranquil setting. The hotel is located in the Gros neighborhood, within walking distance of the beach and the city center.

- **Amenities**: The hotel offers a charming garden, a fitness center, free bike rentals, and well-appointed rooms with classic decor. Breakfast is served daily in the elegant dining room.

- **Special Features**: The hotel's historic charm, combined with modern comforts, provides a unique and pleasant stay for guests.

Hotel Zaragoza Plaza

Hotel Zaragoza Plaza is a budget-friendly option located near La Concha Beach and the city center. The hotel offers clean and comfortable rooms, making it an excellent choice for budget-conscious travelers.

- **Amenities**: The hotel provides free Wi-Fi, a breakfast buffet, and comfortable rooms with modern amenities. The friendly staff is available to assist with travel arrangements and recommendations.

- **Special Features**: The hotel's central location and affordable rates make it a popular choice for both leisure and business travelers.

Budget Accommodation

San Sebastian has several budget-friendly accommodation options that offer great value without compromising on comfort. These options are perfect for travelers looking to save money while enjoying the city's attractions.

Pension Aida

Pension Aida is a family-run guesthouse located in the Gros neighborhood, offering affordable rooms with a cozy atmosphere. The guesthouse is within walking distance of the beach, restaurants, and shops.

- **Amenities**: The guesthouse offers free Wi-Fi, comfortable rooms with shared or private bathrooms, and a communal lounge area. The staff is known for their warm hospitality and helpfulness.
- **Special Features**: The guesthouse's homey atmosphere and convenient location make it a great base for exploring San Sebastian on a budget.

Pension Alameda

Located in the Parte Vieja (Old Town), Pension Alameda offers budget-friendly accommodations in a historic building. The guesthouse provides easy access to the city's top attractions, including pintxos bars and historic sites.

- **Amenities**: The guesthouse offers free Wi-Fi, clean and comfortable rooms with shared or private bathrooms, and a friendly atmosphere. Guests can enjoy exploring the vibrant Old Town right at their doorstep.

- **Special Features**: The central location and affordable rates make Pension Alameda a popular choice for budget travelers who want to be in the heart of the action.

Pension Kaia

Pension Kaia is another budget option located in the Old Town, offering simple and affordable rooms. The guesthouse is close to the beach, restaurants, and nightlife.

- **Amenities**: The guesthouse provides free Wi-Fi, basic rooms with shared or private bathrooms, and a welcoming atmosphere. The staff is available to offer tips on local attractions and dining options.

- **Special Features**: The affordable rates and central location make Pension Kaia a convenient choice for budget-conscious travelers.

Hostels

San Sebastian has a range of hostels that provide affordable and social accommodations, making them a great choice for solo travelers, backpackers, and those looking to meet fellow travelers.

A Room in the City

A Room in the City is a modern and stylish hostel located in the city center, offering a variety of room types, from dormitories to private rooms. The hostel is within walking distance of the beach, shopping areas, and nightlife.

- **Amenities**: The hostel features a communal kitchen, a lounge area, free Wi-Fi, and organized activities. Dormitories have individual lockers, reading lights, and privacy curtains.

- **Special Features**: The hostel's vibrant atmosphere and excellent facilities make it a popular choice for young travelers and those looking to socialize.

Koisi Hostel

Koisi Hostel is a contemporary hostel located in the Antiguo neighborhood, close to Ondarreta Beach and Monte Igueldo. The hostel offers a range of room options, from shared dormitories to private rooms.

- **Amenities**: The hostel provides free Wi-Fi, a communal kitchen, a bar, and a rooftop terrace with views of the city. The staff organizes events and activities to help guests connect and explore the city.

- **Special Features**: The modern design, friendly staff, and social atmosphere make Koisi Hostel a great choice for travelers seeking a fun and affordable stay.

Green Nest Hostel Uba Aterpetxea

Located in a peaceful park area, Green Nest Hostel Uba Aterpetxea offers budget-friendly accommodations with a focus on sustainability. The hostel is a short bus ride from the city center, providing a tranquil retreat after a day of exploring.

- **Amenities**: The hostel features a communal kitchen, a garden, free Wi-Fi, and laundry facilities. Guests can enjoy the outdoor terrace and BBQ area.
- **Special Features**: The eco-friendly focus and serene location make Green Nest Hostel Uba Aterpetxea a unique and affordable option for environmentally conscious travelers.

Airbnb and Vacation Rentals

For those who prefer a more private and home-like experience, Airbnb and vacation rentals offer a wide range of options in San Sebastian. From cozy apartments to spacious villas, there are rentals to suit all tastes and budgets.

Airbnb

San Sebastian has a diverse selection of Airbnb listings, ranging from budget-friendly rooms in shared apartments to luxurious beachfront properties. Airbnb provides the flexibility to choose accommodations that meet your specific needs and preferences.

- **Amenities**: Many Airbnb properties offer amenities such as fully equipped kitchens, Wi-Fi, and washing machines, allowing for a comfortable and convenient stay. Hosts often provide local tips and recommendations to enhance your experience.

- **Special Features**: Staying in an Airbnb allows you to experience San Sebastian like a local, with the opportunity to live in residential neighborhoods and explore hidden gems.

Vacation Rentals

For larger groups or families, vacation rentals can provide the space and amenities needed for a comfortable stay. Websites like Vrbo and Booking.com offer a variety of vacation rental options in San Sebastian.

- **Types of Rentals**: Options include apartments, houses, and villas, many of which are located in prime areas such as La Concha, Gros, and the Old Town. These rentals often come with multiple bedrooms, living areas, and outdoor spaces.

- **Special Features**: Vacation rentals offer the flexibility to cook your meals, enjoy private spaces, and have the comforts of home while traveling.

San Sebastian offers a wide range of accommodation options to suit every traveler's needs and budget. Whether you're looking for the ultimate luxury experience, comfortable mid-range hotels, budget-friendly guesthouses, social hostels, or private vacation rentals, you'll find the perfect place to stay. Each option provides a unique way to experience the charm, culture, and beauty of San Sebastian, ensuring a memorable visit to this stunning coastal city.

Neighborhoods And Districts

San Sebastian, known as Donostia in the Basque language, is a city of vibrant and diverse neighborhoods, each with its own unique charm and character. From the historic streets of the Parte Vieja (Old Town) to the bustling area of Gros, the elegant Antiguo, the central hub of Centro, and the residential Amara, there's something for every visitor to explore and enjoy. Here's a detailed look at these neighborhoods and what makes each one special.

Parte Vieja (Old Town)

History and Character

Parte Vieja, or the Old Town, is the historic heart of San Sebastian. Nestled between Monte Urgull and the Urumea River, this neighborhood is a labyrinth of narrow, cobblestone streets lined with traditional Basque buildings. Parte Vieja is steeped in history, having been largely rebuilt after the city was destroyed in 1813 during the Napoleonic Wars.

Attractions

- **Plaza de la Constitución**: This central square is a focal point of the Old Town, surrounded by colorful buildings with numbered balconies. Historically, it served as a bullring, and today, it is a lively area filled with cafes and bars.

- **San Vicente Church**: One of the oldest buildings in the city, this Gothic-style church dates back to the 16th century and features impressive stained glass windows and a striking altarpiece.

- **Basilica of Saint Mary of the Chorus**: This baroque basilica, built in the 18th century, stands at the foot of Monte Urgull and is known for its ornate facade and beautiful interior.

- **San Telmo Museum**: Located at the base of Monte Urgull, this museum offers insights into Basque culture and history, housed in a 16th-century Dominican convent.

Dining and Nightlife

Parte Vieja is renowned for its culinary scene, particularly its pintxos bars. Here, you can sample a wide variety of these Basque tapas, often served on bread and topped with everything from seafood to Iberian ham.

- **La Cuchara de San Telmo**: Famous for its innovative pintxos and bustling atmosphere.
- **Ganbara**: Known for its traditional pintxos and fresh seafood.
- **A Fuego Negro**: Offers modern and creative takes on traditional Basque cuisine.

Nightlife in Parte Vieja is vibrant, with many bars staying open late into the night. The area is especially lively during festivals such as Semana Grande and the San Sebastian International Film Festival.

Gros

Overview

Gros is a dynamic neighborhood located east of the Urumea River, known for its youthful vibe and surfing culture. It's a hub of activity, particularly around Zurriola Beach, which is popular with surfers and sunbathers alike.

Attractions

- **Zurriola Beach**: A hotspot for surfing, this beach attracts both locals and tourists. It's also a great place for sunbathing, beach volleyball, and taking a leisurely stroll along the promenade.

- **Kursaal Congress Centre**: This modern architectural marvel hosts various cultural events, including concerts, exhibitions, and the prestigious San Sebastian International Film Festival.

- **Sagüés**: The area at the eastern end of Zurriola Beach is known for its relaxed atmosphere and beautiful sunsets. It's a great place for a walk or to enjoy a drink at one of the beachside bars.

Dining and Entertainment

Gros offers a wide range of dining options, from traditional Basque cuisine to international fare.

- **Bodega Donostiarra**: A local favorite for its hearty pintxos and friendly atmosphere.
- **Bar Bergara**: Renowned for its award-winning pintxos.
- **Elosta**: A stylish restaurant offering modern Basque cuisine.

In addition to its vibrant food scene, Gros is known for its lively bars and music venues, making it a great place for nightlife.

Antiguo

Overview

Antiguo is one of San Sebastian's oldest neighborhoods, located west of the city center and characterized by its charming streets, historical buildings, and beautiful beaches. It's a quieter, more residential area compared to Parte Vieja and Gros.

Attractions

- **Ondarreta Beach**: Smaller and more tranquil than La Concha, Ondarreta Beach is perfect for families and those looking to relax by the sea. It's also a great spot for paddleboarding and kayaking.

- **Monte Igueldo**: Take the funicular up to Monte Igueldo for panoramic views of San Sebastian and its coastline. At the top, you'll find an old-fashioned amusement park and several viewpoints.

- **Miramar Palace**: This former royal summer residence offers stunning gardens and views over La Concha Bay. It's a great place for a leisurely walk or a picnic.

Dining and Leisure

Antiguo has a selection of charming cafes, traditional Basque restaurants, and cozy bars.

- **Rekondo**: Known for its extensive wine cellar and delicious Basque cuisine.
- **Txubillo**: A popular spot for pintxos and traditional dishes.
- **Bar Oliyos**: A cozy bar perfect for enjoying a drink with friends.

Antiguo's more relaxed pace makes it an ideal area for leisurely walks and enjoying the scenic beauty of San Sebastian.

Centro

Overview

Centro, or the city center, is the commercial and cultural hub of San Sebastian. It is characterized by its elegant 19th-century architecture, bustling shopping streets, and central location, making it a convenient base for exploring the city.

Attractions

- **Buen Pastor Cathedral**: This neo-Gothic cathedral is a prominent landmark in the city center, known for its towering spire and beautiful interior.

- **Plaza Gipuzkoa**: A charming square with landscaped gardens, ponds, and a bandstand. It's a great place to relax and enjoy the surroundings.

- **Alderdi Eder Gardens**: Located along La Concha Bay, these gardens offer a scenic promenade with views of the beach and Monte Urgull.

Shopping and Dining

Centro is the place to go for shopping, with a mix of high-end boutiques, department stores, and local shops.

- **San Martin Market**: A modern market offering fresh produce, gourmet foods, and a variety of dining options.

- **Calle Mayor**: A lively street lined with shops, cafes, and restaurants.

Dining in Centro offers a mix of traditional Basque cuisine and international options.

- **La Muralla**: Known for its modern Basque dishes and stylish setting.

- **Narru**: Offers innovative cuisine with a focus on local ingredients.

Amara

Overview

Amara is a primarily residential neighborhood located south of the city center. It's known for its green spaces, modern amenities, and family-friendly atmosphere. Amara is less touristy, providing a glimpse into the everyday life of San Sebastian's residents.

Attractions

- **Anoeta Stadium**: Home to Real Sociedad, San Sebastian's football club. Catching a match here offers an exciting experience for sports fans.

- **Cristina Enea Park**: A large, peaceful park perfect for walking, jogging, or simply relaxing. The park features landscaped gardens, a duck pond, and several walking paths.

- **Tabakalera**: This former tobacco factory has been transformed into a contemporary culture center, hosting art exhibitions, film screenings, and workshops.

Dining and Local Life

Amara offers a variety of local dining options, with a focus on traditional Basque cuisine and neighborhood cafes.

- **Arzak**: Although technically located on the border of Amara and Gros, this three-Michelin-starred restaurant offers an exceptional dining experience.
- **Bar Desy**: A local favorite for pintxos and casual dining.

Amara's residential nature makes it a quieter place to stay, ideal for families and those looking to experience a more local side of San Sebastian.

San Sebastian's neighborhoods each offer a unique experience, from the historic charm of Parte Vieja to the vibrant energy of Gros, the elegance of Antiguo, the bustling Centro, and the residential tranquility of Amara. Exploring these diverse districts allows visitors to fully appreciate the rich tapestry of culture, history, and lifestyle that San Sebastian has to offer. Whether you're looking to indulge in world-class cuisine, relax on beautiful beaches, or immerse yourself in local culture, San

Sebastian's neighborhoods provide the perfect setting for an unforgettable visit.

Top Attractions

San Sebastian, or Donostia as it is known in Basque, is a city brimming with cultural richness, natural beauty, and historical significance. Here are some of the top attractions that should be on every visitor's itinerary:

La Concha Beach

Overview

La Concha Beach (Playa de la Concha) is often heralded as one of the most beautiful urban beaches in the world. Situated in the heart of San Sebastian, this crescent-shaped beach stretches for about 1.5 kilometers along the Bay of La Concha, offering stunning views, golden sands, and crystal-clear waters.

Attractions and Activities

- **Swimming and Sunbathing**: The gentle waves and clean waters make La Concha ideal for swimming, while the expansive sandy shore is perfect for sunbathing. During the summer months, the beach is a lively hub of activity with both locals and tourists enjoying the sun.

- **Promenade**: The beach is bordered by a picturesque promenade known as Paseo de la Concha. This walkway is adorned with ornate railings and street lamps, making it a perfect spot for a leisurely stroll or a morning jog. The promenade also features several sculptures and viewpoints where you can admire the panoramic vistas of the bay.

- **Water Sports**: For the more adventurous, La Concha offers various water sports such as kayaking, paddleboarding, and even sailing. Equipment rentals and lessons are available along the beachfront.

- **Isla de Santa Clara**: Situated in the middle of the bay, this small island is accessible by boat or even by swimming during low tide for strong swimmers. The island features a small beach, a lighthouse, and walking trails that offer breathtaking views of the city.

Nearby Attractions

- **Miramar Palace**: Overlooking La Concha Beach, this former royal summer residence offers beautifully landscaped gardens and stunning views of the bay. It's a great spot for a picnic or a leisurely walk.

- **Alderdi Eder Gardens**: Located at the eastern end of the beach, these gardens provide a scenic area to relax with beautifully manicured lawns and vibrant flower beds.

Monte Urgull

Overview

Monte Urgull is a historic hill located at the eastern end of San Sebastian, offering a blend of natural beauty, historical sites, and panoramic views of the city and the bay.

Attractions and Activities

- **Castillo de la Mota**: At the summit of Monte Urgull stands the Castillo de la Mota, a castle dating back to the 12th century. The castle houses a museum that provides insights into the history of San Sebastian and its strategic importance.

- **Sagrado Corazón Statue**: At the highest point of Monte Urgull, you'll find the iconic Sagrado Corazón (Sacred Heart) statue, a 12-meter tall figure of Christ that overlooks the city. The statue is a symbol of protection for the city and offers a magnificent viewpoint.

- **Hiking Trails**: Monte Urgull is crisscrossed with several well-maintained hiking trails that lead through lush greenery and offer various lookout points. These trails are suitable for all fitness levels and provide a peaceful escape from the urban hustle.

- **Military History**: Scattered around the hill are remnants of old military fortifications, including cannons and defensive walls. Informational plaques provide historical context, making it a fascinating exploration for history enthusiasts.

Nearby Attractions

- **Aquarium San Sebastian**: Located at the base of Monte Urgull, the aquarium is a fantastic follow-up visit after exploring the hill. It offers a deep dive into marine life and maritime history.

- **Old Town (Parte Vieja)**: The historic Old Town lies just below Monte Urgull, making it convenient to combine a hike with exploring the narrow streets, pintxos bars, and historic sites of this vibrant neighborhood.

San Telmo Museum

Overview

The San Telmo Museum is dedicated to Basque society, culture, and history. Housed in a former 16th-century Dominican convent, the museum is located at the foot of Monte Urgull in the Old Town.

Exhibits and Collections

- **Permanent Collection**: The museum's permanent collection covers a wide range of topics, including archaeology, ethnography, and fine arts. Highlights include artifacts from the prehistoric era, traditional Basque costumes, and religious art.

- **Temporary Exhibitions**: San Telmo regularly hosts temporary exhibitions that showcase contemporary art, photography, and historical themes relevant to Basque culture.

- **Chapel and Cloister**: The museum retains its original chapel and cloister, which are architectural gems in their own right. The chapel features impressive murals by the Catalan artist Josep Maria Sert, depicting scenes from Basque history.

- **Interactive Displays**: Modern multimedia installations and interactive displays enhance the visitor experience, making the museum educational and engaging for all ages.

Events and Activities

- **Cultural Events**: The museum often hosts cultural events, lectures, and workshops that delve into various aspects of Basque heritage and contemporary issues.

- **Guided Tours**: To gain deeper insights, visitors can join guided tours that are available in several languages. These tours provide expert commentary on the museum's exhibits and the history of the building.

Kursaal Congress Centre

Overview

The Kursaal Congress Centre and Auditorium is a striking modern architectural complex located at the mouth of the Urumea River, facing Zurriola Beach. Designed by the renowned architect Rafael

Moneo, the Kursaal consists of two large translucent cubes that glow at night, symbolizing the meeting point of the sea and the city.

Facilities and Functions

- **Auditorium**: The main auditorium hosts a wide range of performances, including concerts, theater productions, and film screenings. It is also a primary venue for the prestigious San Sebastian International Film Festival.

- **Exhibition Halls**: The Kursaal features several exhibition halls that are used for conferences, trade shows, and cultural exhibitions. These versatile spaces can accommodate events of varying sizes and formats.

- **Restaurants and Cafes**: Within the complex, you'll find fine dining options and casual cafes, providing visitors with a variety of culinary experiences. Notably, the Michelin-starred restaurant Ni Neu offers innovative Basque cuisine with stunning views of the river.

Architectural Significance

The Kursaal's design is a blend of bold modernity and environmental sensitivity. The building's translucent facade allows it to change appearance with the varying light conditions, creating a dynamic and visually captivating structure. It has won numerous architectural awards and is considered a landmark of contemporary architecture.

Events and Activities

- **San Sebastian International Film Festival**: Held annually in September, this film festival attracts international stars and cinephiles, making it one of the city's most significant cultural events.

- **Concerts and Performances**: The Kursaal regularly hosts performances by world-renowned artists, orchestras, and theater companies, offering a rich cultural calendar year-round.

Aquarium San Sebastian

Overview

Aquarium San Sebastian, located at the edge of the Old Town and at the base of Monte Urgull, is one of the most visited attractions in the city. It offers a fascinating journey through the marine world, combining historical exhibits with live marine displays.

Exhibits and Features

- **Oceanarium**: The centerpiece of the aquarium is the impressive 360-degree oceanarium, which features a transparent tunnel allowing visitors to walk through and experience marine life up close. Sharks, rays, and a variety of fish species swim overhead, providing a captivating underwater experience.

- **Marine Biodiversity**: The aquarium showcases the rich marine biodiversity of the Bay of Biscay, with exhibits on local species such as octopuses, seahorses, and jellyfish. Interactive displays and educational panels provide insights into the marine ecosystem.

- **Maritime History**: In addition to live marine exhibits, the aquarium houses a maritime museum that delves into the naval history of San Sebastian and the Basque Country. Artifacts include ship models, navigational instruments, and historical documents.

- **Tropical Exhibits**: The aquarium also features tropical exhibits with colorful coral reefs and exotic fish species from around the world, offering a contrast to the local marine life.

Educational Programs

- **Workshops and Tours**: The aquarium offers educational workshops and guided tours for visitors of all ages, enhancing their understanding of marine conservation and the importance of protecting ocean habitats.

- **Children's Activities**: Special programs and activities designed for children include interactive exhibits, touch tanks, and storytelling sessions, making it an engaging visit for families.

Conservation Efforts

Aquarium San Sebastian is actively involved in marine conservation efforts, participating in research projects and initiatives aimed at preserving marine biodiversity. Visitors can learn about these efforts and how they can contribute to protecting the oceans.

San Sebastian's top attractions offer a diverse array of experiences, from the natural beauty and leisure activities of La Concha Beach to the historical significance of Monte Urgull, the cultural richness of the San Telmo Museum, the modern architectural marvel of the Kursaal Congress Centre, and the fascinating marine world of the Aquarium San Sebastian. Each attraction provides a unique perspective on the city's heritage, culture, and natural environment, making San Sebastian a truly captivating destination. Whether you're interested in history, architecture, marine life, or simply soaking up the sun on one of Europe's most beautiful beaches, San Sebastian has something for everyone to enjoy.

Cultural Experiences

San Sebastian, known locally as Donostia, is a city deeply rooted in Basque culture, rich traditions, and vibrant arts. From age-old festivals to contemporary art galleries, San Sebastian offers a wealth of cultural experiences that reflect its unique heritage and dynamic spirit. Here's an in-depth look at what you can explore:

Basque Culture and Traditions

Overview

The Basque Country, or Euskal Herria, is a region with a distinct cultural identity that spans parts of northern Spain and southwestern France. San Sebastian, as one of its major cities, is a hub for Basque traditions, language, and customs.

Language

Euskara (Basque) is one of the oldest languages in Europe and is spoken by a significant portion of San Sebastian's population. Unlike Spanish and French, Euskara has no known linguistic relatives. Many signs in the city are bilingual, in both Spanish and Basque, and locals take pride in preserving and promoting their language.

Cuisine

Basque cuisine is renowned worldwide, and San Sebastian is its culinary capital. Key elements of Basque cuisine include:

- **Pintxos**: These are small snacks typically served in bars, similar to tapas but often more elaborate. Pintxos bars line the streets of the Parte Vieja (Old Town), each offering a variety of unique and flavorful bites.

- **Txakoli**: A young, slightly sparkling white wine that is traditionally served with pintxos. Txakoli is a staple in Basque culinary culture.

- **Seafood**: Given its coastal location, San Sebastian boasts some of the freshest seafood. Dishes like grilled fish, squid, and seafood stews are common.

Sports

Pelota, or Basque handball, is a traditional sport played in San Sebastian. The sport is similar to squash but played with bare hands or a wooden bat. Matches can be seen at local frontons (courts), and it's a sport that symbolizes Basque strength and agility.

Traditional Clothing

Basque traditional clothing is often showcased during festivals and cultural events. Women typically wear long skirts, white blouses, and aprons, while men don berets (boinas), white shirts, and sashes. These outfits are not just costumes but represent a deep respect for cultural heritage.

Local Festivals and Events

San Sebastian is known for its vibrant festivals that celebrate everything from film to music to local traditions. These events are central to the city's cultural calendar and draw visitors from around the world.

San Sebastian International Film Festival

Held annually in September, the San Sebastian International Film Festival (SSIFF) is one of the most prestigious film festivals in the world. It features screenings of international films, red carpet events, and awards such as the Golden Shell for the best film. The festival attracts famous actors, directors, and film enthusiasts, making it a highlight of the cultural year.

Semana Grande (Aste Nagusia)

Semana Grande, or "Big Week," takes place in August and is San Sebastian's largest festival. The week-long event features:

- **Fireworks**: Nightly fireworks displays that light up the sky over La Concha Bay, part of an international fireworks competition.
- **Traditional Sports**: Demonstrations of Basque rural sports such as stone lifting, wood chopping, and rowing.

- **Parades and Concerts**: Daily parades, live music, and performances throughout the city.
- **Cattle Fair**: A traditional cattle fair that highlights Basque agricultural practices.

Tamborrada

Celebrated on January 20th, Tamborrada is a drumming festival honoring the city's patron saint, San Sebastián. The festival involves:

- **Parades**: Thousands of residents, dressed in traditional costumes of cooks and soldiers, parade through the streets, drumming and singing.
- **24-hour Celebration**: The festivities start at midnight and continue for 24 hours, with various drumming groups performing throughout the city.
- **Children's Tamborrada**: During the day, children participate in their own drumming

parades, reflecting the community's effort to pass on traditions to younger generations.

La Semana del Cine Fantástico y de Terror (Horror and Fantasy Film Week)

This unique film festival, held in late October or early November, focuses on horror and fantasy genres. It features screenings, discussions, and themed events, attracting fans of genre cinema and providing a platform for both established and emerging filmmakers.

Art Galleries and Museums

San Sebastian is home to several art galleries and museums that showcase both traditional and contemporary art, providing insight into the region's artistic heritage and current trends.

San Telmo Museum

Located at the foot of Monte Urgull, the San Telmo Museum is dedicated to Basque society and history. The museum's collections include:

- **Historical Artifacts**: Items from the prehistoric era to modern times, highlighting Basque cultural and social evolution.
- **Art Exhibitions**: Works by Basque artists, including sculptures, paintings, and installations.
- **Chapel Murals**: Impressive murals by Josep Maria Sert, depicting scenes from Basque history and culture.

Tabakalera

Tabakalera is a contemporary culture center housed in a former tobacco factory. It serves as a hub for creative activities, offering:

- **Art Exhibitions**: Rotating exhibits featuring contemporary artists from the Basque Country and beyond.

- **Film Screenings**: An extensive program of independent and experimental films.

- **Workshops and Studios**: Spaces for artists to work and for visitors to participate in creative workshops.

- **Events**: Regular events including talks, performances, and festivals focused on various aspects of contemporary culture.

Kursaal Congress Centre

The Kursaal Congress Centre not only hosts events and performances but also features art exhibitions in its public spaces. The striking architecture of the building itself, designed by Rafael Moneo, is considered a work of art.

Eduardo Chillida's Works

San Sebastian is closely associated with Eduardo Chillida, one of Spain's most famous sculptors. His works can be seen throughout the city, most notably:

- **Peine del Viento (Comb of the Wind)**: A series of sculptures located at the end of Ondarreta Beach, integrated with the natural landscape to create a powerful artistic statement.
- **Chillida-Leku**: Just outside San Sebastian, this museum dedicated to Chillida's work features an extensive collection of his sculptures in a beautiful garden setting.

Music and Performing Arts

San Sebastian has a vibrant music and performing arts scene, with events and venues that cater to a wide range of tastes.

Jazzaldia

The San Sebastian Jazz Festival, or Jazzaldia, is held every July and is one of Europe's oldest jazz festivals. It features:

- **International Artists**: Performances by renowned jazz musicians from around the world.

- **Diverse Venues**: Concerts held in various locations, including the Kursaal Auditorium, outdoor stages, and even on the beach.

- **Free Concerts**: Many performances are free, making jazz accessible to a broad audience.

Victoria Eugenia Theatre

This historic theater, located in the city center, hosts a variety of performances including:

- **Theatre Productions**: Classic and contemporary plays performed by local and international theater companies.

- **Dance**: Ballet and modern dance performances.

- **Concerts**: A diverse range of musical performances, from classical to contemporary genres.

Basque Music

San Sebastian is a great place to experience traditional Basque music, which includes:

- **Txistu and Tamboril**: Traditional Basque flute and drum music, often heard during festivals and celebrations.
- **Choirs and Folk Groups**: Performances by local choirs and folk groups, showcasing the region's vocal traditions and folk dances.

Donostia Kultura

Donostia Kultura is an organization that coordinates cultural activities in the city, offering a year-round program of:

- **Concerts**: Regular music performances ranging from classical to modern.

- **Theater and Dance**: A wide array of performing arts events.

- **Workshops and Classes**: Opportunities for residents and visitors to engage in cultural activities, learn new skills, and participate in the arts.

San Sebastian's rich cultural tapestry offers something for every visitor, from the deep-rooted traditions of Basque culture to vibrant festivals, diverse art galleries, and a dynamic music and performing arts scene. Whether you're strolling through a museum, enjoying a pintxo in the Old Town, or attending a world-class festival, San Sebastian's cultural experiences are sure to leave a lasting impression. This city not only preserves its unique heritage but also embraces contemporary creativity, making it a must-visit destination for culture enthusiasts.

Outdoor Activities

San Sebastian, with its stunning natural landscape and coastal location, offers a plethora of outdoor activities for visitors to enjoy. From its beautiful beaches and thrilling water sports to scenic hiking trails, cycling routes, and serene parks and gardens, there's something for everyone looking to embrace the great outdoors. Here's a detailed guide to the top outdoor activities in San Sebastian.

Beaches and Water Sports

La Concha Beach

Overview

La Concha Beach, often hailed as one of the most beautiful urban beaches in the world, is the crown jewel of San Sebastian. Its crescent-shaped bay, soft golden sands, and clear waters make it a perfect spot for relaxation and recreation.

Activities

- **Swimming and Sunbathing**: The gentle waves and clean waters are ideal for swimming, while the expansive sandy beach is perfect for sunbathing.
- **Kayaking and Paddleboarding**: Equipment rentals are available along the

beachfront. Paddleboarding across the calm bay is a popular activity, offering a unique perspective of the city.

- **Beach Volleyball**: There are several courts set up along the beach, providing an opportunity for some friendly competition.

Ondarreta Beach

Overview

Located to the west of La Concha Beach, Ondarreta Beach is smaller and more tranquil. It's a family-friendly beach with shallow waters and a relaxed atmosphere.

Activities

- **Swimming and Sunbathing**: Like La Concha, Ondarreta offers excellent conditions for swimming and sunbathing.

- **Sandcastle Building**: The fine sand makes it ideal for building sandcastles, a favorite activity among children.

- **Tennis and Volleyball**: The beach has facilities for beach tennis and volleyball, providing more options for active visitors.

Zurriola Beach

Overview

Zurriola Beach, located in the Gros neighborhood, is the go-to spot for surfers and young people. The beach is known for its consistent waves, making it a hotspot for surfing enthusiasts.

Activities

- **Surfing**: With several surf schools and rental shops nearby, Zurriola is perfect for both beginners and experienced surfers.

- **Bodyboarding and Kite Surfing**: The beach's waves are also ideal for bodyboarding and kite surfing.

- **Beach Soccer**: During the summer, you'll often find beach soccer tournaments and pick-up games taking place on the sand.

Hiking and Nature Walks

Monte Urgull

Overview

Monte Urgull is a historic hill located at the eastern end of San Sebastian. It offers a combination of natural beauty, panoramic views, and historical landmarks.

Hiking Trails

- **Castillo de la Mota**: At the summit, you'll find the Castillo de la Mota, a castle dating back to the 12th century. The hike up offers stunning views of the city and bay.

- **Sagrado Corazón Statue**: This iconic statue of Christ stands at the top of Monte Urgull, providing an impressive viewpoint over San Sebastian.

- **Scenic Pathways**: The hill is crisscrossed with well-maintained paths, perfect for leisurely walks amidst lush greenery and historical sites.

Monte Igueldo

Overview

Monte Igueldo is another prominent hill in San Sebastian, located to the west of the city. It offers breathtaking views and an old-fashioned amusement park at its summit.

Hiking Trails

- **Funicular Ride**: You can take the funicular railway to the top for a scenic and unique experience.

- **Walking Paths**: Several trails wind their way up Monte Igueldo, offering beautiful vistas and a more challenging hike.

- **Amusement Park**: At the top, the amusement park features vintage rides and attractions, making it a fun destination for families.

Paseo Nuevo

Overview

Paseo Nuevo is a scenic coastal path that wraps around Monte Urgull, providing stunning views of the sea and city.

Activities

- **Walking and Jogging**: The wide, paved path is ideal for a leisurely walk or a brisk jog, with the sound of waves crashing against the rocks providing a soothing backdrop.

- **Photography**: The dramatic coastal scenery makes it a great spot for photography, especially during sunset.

Cycling Routes

Bidegorris

Overview

San Sebastian is a bike-friendly city with an extensive network of dedicated cycling paths known as bidegorris. These paths connect key areas of the city and provide a safe and scenic way to explore.

Popular Routes

- **La Concha Promenade**: Cycling along the promenade offers stunning views of the beach and bay, making it one of the most popular routes.

- **Gros to Antiguo**: This route takes you through the vibrant Gros neighborhood, past Zurriola Beach, and along the river to the Antiguo district.
- **River Urumea Path**: A scenic route that follows the Urumea River, offering a peaceful ride through lush green areas.

Bike Rentals

Overview

There are several bike rental shops throughout San Sebastian, making it easy to find a bike that suits your needs.

- **Dbizi**: The city's bike-sharing system, with numerous stations throughout the city. You can rent bikes by the hour or for longer periods.

- **Private Rental Shops**: Various shops offer standard bikes, electric bikes, and even tandem bikes for rent. Some popular options include La Bicicleta and Donostibike.

Parks and Gardens

Cristina Enea Park

Overview

Cristina Enea Park is one of San Sebastian's largest and most beautiful parks, located near the city center. It offers a serene escape from the urban hustle and bustle.

Features

- **Walking Paths**: The park features several winding paths through lush greenery, perfect for a leisurely stroll or jog.

- **Wildlife**: You'll find a variety of birds, ducks, and even peacocks roaming the park, adding to its charm.

- **Gardens**: The park's well-maintained gardens are filled with vibrant flowers and provide peaceful spots to relax and enjoy nature.

Miramar Palace Gardens

Overview

Situated between La Concha Beach and Ondarreta Beach, the gardens of Miramar Palace offer stunning views of the bay and a tranquil environment.

Features

- **Landscaped Gardens**: The beautifully landscaped gardens feature manicured lawns, flower beds, and shaded areas perfect for picnics.

- **Historical Significance**: The palace was once the summer residence of the Spanish royal family, adding a touch of historical significance to your visit.

- **Walking Trails**: Several walking trails wind through the gardens, offering scenic views and a peaceful setting.

Alderdi Eder Gardens

Overview

Located along La Concha Bay, Alderdi Eder Gardens are a beautifully landscaped park area that offers a perfect blend of natural beauty and city views.

Features

- **Flower Beds**: The gardens are known for their colorful flower beds, which change with the seasons.

- **Benches and Pathways**: Numerous benches and pathways make it a great place for a leisurely stroll or to sit and enjoy the view.

- **Playground**: There is a small playground for children, making it a family-friendly destination.

Parque de Aiete

Overview

A bit further from the city center, Parque de Aiete is a tranquil park surrounding the Aiete Palace. It's a peaceful spot perfect for nature lovers.

Features

- **Wooded Areas**: The park has extensive wooded areas with walking paths that offer a refreshing escape into nature.

- **Pond**: A small pond adds to the park's serene atmosphere, providing a habitat for ducks and other wildlife.

- **Aiete Palace**: The park is centered around the historic Aiete Palace, adding a touch of elegance to the natural setting.

San Sebastian's outdoor activities offer something for everyone, whether you're a beach lover, an adventure seeker, a cyclist, or someone looking to enjoy a peaceful walk in a beautiful park. The city's natural beauty and well-maintained recreational areas provide ample opportunities to explore and enjoy the great outdoors. Whether you're surfing the waves at Zurriola Beach, hiking up Monte Urgull, cycling along scenic routes, or relaxing in one of the city's many parks and gardens, San Sebastian is a haven for outdoor enthusiasts.

Culinary Delights

San Sebastian, or Donostia, is a gastronomic paradise known for its rich culinary heritage and vibrant food scene. The city offers a wide range of dining experiences, from casual pintxos bars to Michelin-starred restaurants, traditional Basque cuisine, and bustling food markets. Here's a detailed guide to the culinary delights you can enjoy in San Sebastian.

Pintxos Bars

Overview

Pintxos (pronounced "peen-chos") are small, flavorful snacks that are a staple of Basque cuisine. Typically served in bars and taverns, pintxos are the perfect way to sample a variety of flavors and ingredients in one meal. San Sebastian is renowned for its pintxos bars, particularly in the Parte Vieja (Old Town) and Gros neighborhoods.

Top Pintxos Bars

Bar La Cuchara de San Telmo

Located in the heart of the Old Town, Bar La Cuchara de San Telmo is a must-visit for pintxos lovers. Known for its innovative takes on traditional dishes, this bar offers an array of mouthwatering options.

- **Specialties**: Try the grilled foie gras, pig's ear, and octopus with potato puree. Each dish is expertly prepared and bursting with flavor.

Bar Ganbara

A family-run establishment, Bar Ganbara is famed for its use of fresh, high-quality ingredients. It's a favorite among locals and tourists alike.

- **Specialties**: Don't miss the mushroom pintxos with egg yolk, the crab tart, and the Iberian ham. The bar also offers a selection of excellent wines to complement your meal.

Bar Txepetxa

For seafood enthusiasts, Bar Txepetxa is the place to be. This bar specializes in anchovy pintxos, prepared in a variety of delicious ways.

- **Specialties**: The anchovy pintxos with foie gras, blueberry jam, or sea urchin are particularly popular. The creative combinations are sure to surprise and delight your taste buds.

Pintxos Etiquette

When visiting pintxos bars, it's common to order a drink (usually a small beer, cider, or wine) and a few pintxos at each stop, moving from bar to bar to sample different offerings. It's a social and relaxed way of dining, perfect for experiencing the local food culture.

Traditional Basque Cuisine

Overview

Basque cuisine is known for its simplicity, high-quality ingredients, and robust flavors. Traditional Basque dishes often feature seafood, meats, vegetables, and beans, reflecting the region's coastal and agricultural heritage.

Key Dishes

Bacalao a la Vizcaína

This traditional dish consists of salted cod cooked in a rich sauce made from red peppers, onions, tomatoes, and garlic. It's a hearty and flavorful meal that showcases the region's love for seafood.

Marmitako

Originally a fisherman's stew, marmitako is made with tuna, potatoes, onions, peppers, and tomatoes. It's a comforting dish, perfect for warming up on a cool day by the sea.

Txangurro

Txangurro is a classic Basque dish made with spider crab. The crab meat is sautéed with onions, leeks, tomatoes, and brandy, then baked in the crab shell. It's a luxurious and flavorful dish often enjoyed as a special treat.

Talo

A traditional Basque corn flatbread, talo is often served with chistorra (a type of Basque sausage) or cheese. It's a popular street food, especially during festivals and fairs.

Where to Try Traditional Basque Cuisine

Restaurante Arzak

A three-Michelin-starred restaurant, Arzak offers a modern take on traditional Basque cuisine. Run by the father-daughter team of Juan Mari and Elena Arzak, the restaurant is renowned for its innovative dishes and impeccable service.

- **Specialties**: The tasting menu features a variety of creative dishes that highlight local ingredients and flavors.

Asador Etxebarri

Located in the Atxondo Valley, about an hour's drive from San Sebastian, Asador Etxebarri is famous for its wood-fired cooking. Chef Victor Arguinzoniz uses traditional techniques to create simple, yet extraordinary dishes.

- **Specialties**: The grilled meat and seafood are exceptional, with flavors enhanced by the unique smoky aroma from the wood fire.

Michelin-Starred Restaurants

Overview

San Sebastian boasts more Michelin stars per capita than anywhere else in the world, making it a top destination for fine dining enthusiasts. The city is home to several renowned restaurants that offer exquisite dining experiences.

Top Michelin-Starred Restaurants

Mugaritz

Located in the hills outside San Sebastian, Mugaritz is a two-Michelin-starred restaurant known for its avant-garde cuisine. Chef Andoni Luis Aduriz creates dishes that challenge traditional culinary boundaries.

- **Experience**: Dining at Mugaritz is an immersive experience, with a tasting menu that includes around 20 inventive courses. Each dish is designed to provoke thought and delight the senses.

Akelarre

Perched on Monte Igueldo with stunning views of the sea, Akelarre is a three-Michelin-starred restaurant led by Chef Pedro Subijana. The restaurant offers a combination of exceptional food and breathtaking scenery.

- **Specialties**: The tasting menu features dishes that blend traditional Basque flavors with modern techniques. The sea urchin custard and charcoal-grilled pigeon are particularly notable.

Martin Berasategui

Located in nearby Lasarte-Oria, Martin Berasategui's eponymous restaurant holds three

Michelin stars and is known for its innovative and meticulously crafted dishes.

- **Specialties**: The tasting menu showcases a range of exquisite dishes, including the iconic mille-feuille of smoked eel and the red mullet with edible scales.

Food Markets and Culinary Tours

Overview

Exploring San Sebastian's food markets and taking part in culinary tours are excellent ways to experience the local food culture and discover the best of Basque cuisine.

Top Food Markets

La Bretxa Market

Located in the heart of the Old Town, La Bretxa Market is one of San Sebastian's most famous food markets. It offers a wide variety of fresh produce, meats, seafood, and artisanal products.

- **Highlights**: The market is known for its high-quality seafood, including fresh fish, shellfish, and octopus. Local vendors also sell traditional Basque cheeses, cured meats, and seasonal vegetables.

San Martin Market

San Martin Market is a modern indoor market located in the Centro neighborhood. It's a great place to find fresh produce, gourmet foods, and local delicacies.

- **Highlights**: In addition to fresh fruits and vegetables, the market features stalls selling artisanal breads, pastries, and prepared foods. There are also several cafes and eateries where you can enjoy a meal or snack.

Culinary Tours

Participating in a culinary tour is a fantastic way to explore San Sebastian's food scene, learn about Basque cuisine, and taste a variety of local specialties.

Devour Tours

Devour Tours offers guided food tours that take you through the best pintxos bars, markets, and eateries in San Sebastian. The tours are led by knowledgeable guides who share insights into the city's culinary traditions and history.

- **Tour Highlights**: The San Sebastian Food Tour includes stops at iconic pintxos bars, a visit to La Bretxa Market, and tastings of local wines and delicacies.

Mimo Bite the Experience

Mimo Bite the Experience offers a range of culinary experiences, including cooking classes, market tours, and gourmet tastings. Their San

Sebastian Market Tour and Cooking Class is particularly popular.

- **Tour Highlights**: The tour includes a guided visit to San Martin Market, followed by a hands-on cooking class where you'll learn to prepare traditional Basque dishes.

Cooking Classes

For those who want to dive deeper into Basque cuisine, taking a cooking class is a great way to learn the techniques and recipes from local chefs.

San Sebastian Food Cooking School

Located in the heart of the city, San Sebastian Food Cooking School offers a variety of classes that cover everything from pintxos to traditional Basque dishes. The classes are hands-on and suitable for all skill levels.

- **Class Highlights**: The Pintxos Cooking Class teaches you how to create classic pintxos, while the Basque Cooking Class covers traditional dishes like bacalao a la vizcaína and txangurro.

San Sebastian's culinary delights are a testament to its rich cultural heritage and innovative spirit. From the bustling pintxos bars and traditional Basque cuisine to the world-renowned Michelin-starred restaurants and vibrant food markets, the city offers a gastronomic experience like no other. Whether you're savoring pintxos in the Old Town, dining at a fine restaurant with a view of the sea, or exploring the local markets, San Sebastian promises a culinary journey that will delight your senses and leave you with unforgettable memories.

Nightlife and Entertainment

San Sebastian, or Donostia, is renowned not only for its beautiful landscapes and culinary excellence but also for its vibrant nightlife and entertainment scene. The city offers a diverse range of options for evening activities, from lively bars and pubs to energetic nightclubs, live music venues, and cultural theaters and cinemas. Here's a detailed guide to the best nightlife and entertainment experiences in San Sebastian.

Bars and Pubs

Overview

San Sebastian's bar scene is eclectic, offering everything from traditional Basque bars to trendy cocktail lounges and cozy pubs. The Old Town (Parte Vieja) and Gros neighborhoods are particularly popular for bar hopping, but you'll find great spots throughout the city.

Top Bars and Pubs

Bar Zeruko

Located in the Old Town, Bar Zeruko is famous for its innovative pintxos and vibrant atmosphere. It's a perfect place to start your night with some creative bites and a glass of txakoli (a local sparkling white wine).

- **Specialties**: Try the "La Hoguera," a smoked cod pintxo that you cook yourself at the table, and the "Tarta de Queso," a delicious cheesecake pintxo.

La Taberna de Blas

Situated in the Gros neighborhood, La Taberna de Blas is a popular bar known for its extensive selection of wines and relaxed vibe. It's a great spot for enjoying a few drinks with friends.

- **Specialties**: The bar offers a wide variety of local and international wines, as well as a good selection of craft beers.

Sir Winston Churchill Pub

For those who enjoy a more traditional pub atmosphere, the Sir Winston Churchill Pub, located near the city center, is a great choice. This English-style pub offers a cozy environment and a wide selection of beers and spirits.

- **Specialties**: The pub serves classic British pub fare like fish and chips, along with a variety of ales and whiskies.

Bar Hopping

Bar hopping is a popular activity in San Sebastian, especially in the Old Town where the streets are lined with bars offering delicious pintxos and drinks. It's common to move from one bar to the next, sampling different specialties along the way.

Nightclubs

Overview

San Sebastian's nightlife extends well into the early hours, with several nightclubs offering a place to dance and enjoy music until dawn. The city's nightclubs cater to a range of musical tastes, from electronic dance music to hip-hop and reggaeton.

Top Nightclubs

Bataplan Disco

Located along La Concha Bay, Bataplan Disco is one of the city's most iconic nightclubs. With its beachfront location and stylish interior, Bataplan attracts a trendy crowd and offers a mix of electronic, house, and pop music.

- **Specialties**: The club features top local and international DJs, themed parties, and stunning views of the bay from its terrace.

GU San Sebastian

Situated near the Kursaal Congress Centre, GU San Sebastian is a sophisticated nightclub known for its chic ambiance and high-energy dance floor. The club offers a variety of music genres, from house and techno to commercial hits.

- **Specialties**: GU often hosts special events and guest DJs, providing a dynamic nightlife experience.

Dabadaba

For those seeking a more alternative and eclectic nightlife experience, Dabadaba in the Egia neighborhood is the place to be. Known for its indie, rock, and electronic music, Dabadaba is a favorite among the local hipster crowd.

- **Specialties**: In addition to live DJ sets, the club hosts live concerts, film screenings, and art exhibitions, making it a cultural hotspot as well as a nightclub.

Live Music Venues

Overview

San Sebastian boasts a thriving live music scene, with venues ranging from intimate bars to large concert halls. The city hosts performances in a variety of genres, including jazz, rock, classical, and traditional Basque music.

Top Live Music Venues

Victoria Eugenia Theatre

Victoria Eugenia Theatre, a historic and beautifully restored venue in the heart of the city, is one of San Sebastian's premier locations for live music. It hosts a variety of performances, including classical concerts, opera, and jazz.

- **Specialties**: The theatre is a key venue for the San Sebastian Jazz Festival (Jazzaldia) and often features internationally renowned artists.

Kursaal Congress Centre

The Kursaal Congress Centre is another major venue for live music in San Sebastian. This modern architectural landmark hosts concerts, festivals, and cultural events throughout the year.

- **Specialties**: The Kursaal is known for its excellent acoustics and hosts performances by top orchestras, bands, and solo artists. It's also a primary venue for the San Sebastian International Film Festival.

Altxerri

For a more intimate live music experience, Altxerri is a must-visit. Located in the city center, this underground jazz club offers live jazz, blues, and soul music in a cozy and atmospheric setting.

- **Specialties**: The club features both local and international musicians and is known for its relaxed vibe and quality performances.

Le Bukowski

Le Bukowski, located in the Egia neighborhood, is a vibrant music venue and bar that hosts live concerts, DJ sets, and themed nights. It's popular among the younger crowd and those looking for a lively night out.

- **Specialties**: The venue covers a wide range of music genres, from rock and punk to electronic and hip-hop.

Theaters and Cinemas

Overview

San Sebastian has a rich cultural scene that includes several theaters and cinemas offering a variety of performances and screenings. Whether you're interested in seeing a classic play, a contemporary dance performance, or the latest film, there are plenty of options to choose from.

Top Theaters

Victoria Eugenia Theatre

As mentioned earlier, Victoria Eugenia Theatre is not only a venue for live music but also hosts a range of theatrical performances, including plays, dance, and opera.

- **Specialties**: The theatre's grand architecture and historical significance make it a key cultural venue in San Sebastian. It regularly hosts international theater productions and ballet performances.

Principal Theatre

Principal Theatre, located in the Old Town, is one of the oldest theaters in San Sebastian. It offers a diverse program of plays, musicals, and dance performances.

- **Specialties**: The theater is particularly known for hosting the opening and closing ceremonies of the San Sebastian International Film Festival, as well as a variety of local and touring productions.

Top Cinemas

Cines Trueba

Cines Trueba, located in the Gros neighborhood, is a modern cinema complex that screens a mix of mainstream, independent, and international films. It's a great place to catch the latest releases as well as special screenings of classic films.

- **Specialties**: The cinema often hosts film festivals and special events, providing a platform for independent and foreign films.

Cines Príncipe

Cines Príncipe, situated in the city center, is another popular cinema that offers a wide selection of films. With multiple screens and comfortable seating, it's a favorite spot for moviegoers.

- **Specialties**: The cinema is known for its diverse film programming, including art-house films and movies in their original language with subtitles.

Outdoor Cinema

During the summer months, San Sebastian hosts outdoor cinema events, where classic and contemporary films are screened in beautiful open-air settings. Locations such as Zurriola Beach and the Alderdi Eder Gardens provide stunning backdrops for these cinematic experiences.

- **Specialties**: These events are often free and attract large audiences, making them a great way to enjoy a movie under the stars while experiencing the city's vibrant atmosphere.

San Sebastian's nightlife and entertainment scene is as diverse and vibrant as the city itself. Whether you're looking to enjoy a few drinks at a cozy pub, dance the night away at a trendy nightclub, listen to live music, or catch a theater performance or film, there's something for everyone. The city's lively bars and pubs offer a taste of local culture and camaraderie, while its nightclubs provide energetic spaces for dancing and socializing. Live music venues cater to a wide range of tastes, from jazz and classical to rock and electronic, ensuring memorable experiences for music lovers. Theaters and cinemas round out the city's cultural offerings, providing a rich tapestry of performances and screenings that highlight San Sebastian's commitment to the arts. Whether you're a night owl or a culture enthusiast, San Sebastian's nightlife and entertainment options are sure to leave you with lasting memories.

Shopping

San Sebastian, with its charming blend of traditional Basque culture and modern sophistication, offers a delightful shopping experience. From bustling local markets and unique boutique stores to contemporary shopping malls and artisan shops, the city provides an array of options for every type of shopper. Here's a detailed guide to the best shopping spots in San Sebastian.

Local Markets

La Bretxa Market

Overview

La Bretxa Market, located in the heart of the Old Town (Parte Vieja), is one of San Sebastian's most iconic markets. It's a vibrant spot where locals and tourists alike come to buy fresh produce, seafood, meats, and other gourmet delights.

What to Buy

- **Fresh Seafood**: San Sebastian's proximity to the sea ensures that La Bretxa offers some of the freshest seafood available. Look for fish, shellfish, and octopus.
- **Local Produce**: The market is filled with stalls selling fresh fruits, vegetables, and herbs.

Seasonal produce like piquillo peppers and asparagus are must-tries.

- **Basque Specialties**: You can find traditional Basque products such as Idiazabal cheese, chorizo, and jamón (ham).

Shopping Tips

- **Morning Visit**: The market is most vibrant in the morning, so aim to visit early for the best selection of goods.

- **Interacting with Vendors**: Don't hesitate to chat with the friendly vendors, who are often more than willing to share cooking tips and offer samples.

San Martin Market

Overview

San Martin Market is a modern indoor market located in the Centro neighborhood. It combines traditional market stalls with contemporary retail spaces, providing a diverse shopping experience.

What to Buy

- **Gourmet Foods**: The market offers a wide variety of gourmet foods, including artisanal breads, pastries, and chocolates.

- **Fresh Produce**: Similar to La Bretxa, San Martin has an excellent selection of fresh fruits, vegetables, and seafood.

- **Prepared Foods**: There are several stalls selling ready-to-eat foods, perfect for a quick lunch or snack while shopping.

Shopping Tips

- **Sampling**: Take advantage of the free samples offered by many vendors to try before you buy.

- **Cafes and Restaurants**: The market has several cafes and restaurants where you can take a break and enjoy a meal.

Boutique Stores

Overview

San Sebastian's boutique stores offer unique and high-quality products, from fashion and accessories to home decor and gifts. The city's boutique scene is concentrated in the Old Town, Gros, and Centro neighborhoods.

Top Boutique Stores

Aitor Lasa Gaztategia

Overview

Aitor Lasa Gaztategia is a gourmet food shop specializing in Basque cheeses and other delicacies. Located in the Old Town, it's a haven for food enthusiasts.

What to Buy

- **Cheeses**: The shop offers an extensive selection of Basque cheeses, including Id iazabal and Roncal. The knowledgeable staff can help you choose the perfect cheese for your taste.

- **Cured Meats**: Find a variety of cured meats, including chorizo and jamón ibérico, perfect for creating your own pintxos at home.
- **Local Delicacies**: The shop also stocks other Basque specialties like anchovies, preserves, and artisanal olive oils.

Eguzkilore

Overview

Eguzkilore is a boutique jewelry store that offers unique pieces inspired by Basque culture and traditions. Located in the city center, it's a great place to find a special keepsake.

What to Buy

- **Jewelry**: The store's signature pieces are inspired by the Eguzkilore flower, a symbol of protection in Basque mythology. Look for necklaces, bracelets, and rings featuring this motif.

- **Craftsmanship**: Each piece is crafted with attention to detail, making it a perfect gift or personal treasure.

Arkaitza

Overview

Located in the Gros neighborhood, Arkaitza is a boutique that showcases contemporary Basque fashion and design. It's known for its stylish and innovative offerings.

What to Buy

- **Fashion**: The store offers a range of clothing and accessories from local designers, including unique Basque berets and modern takes on traditional garments.

- **Home Decor**: Find beautifully designed home goods, from ceramics to textiles, that bring a touch of Basque artistry to your home.

Shopping Malls

Overview

For a more comprehensive shopping experience, San Sebastian has several modern shopping malls that offer a variety of stores, from high-end fashion to everyday essentials.

Top Shopping Malls

Centro Comercial San Martín

Overview

Centro Comercial San Martín is a modern shopping mall located near the San Martin Market. It's a multi-level complex with a wide range of shops, eateries, and services.

What to Buy

- **Fashion**: The mall features several international and local fashion brands, offering the latest trends and styles.

- **Beauty and Health**: Find a variety of beauty products, skincare items, and health services.

- **Books and Electronics**: The mall also has bookstores and electronics stores, making it a one-stop shop for all your needs.

Shopping Tips

- **Special Offers**: Keep an eye out for seasonal sales and promotions, especially during the summer and winter months.

- **Food Court**: Take a break at the food court, which offers a variety of dining options from quick snacks to full meals.

Garbera Shopping Centre

Overview

Located on the outskirts of San Sebastian, Garbera Shopping Centre is one of the largest malls in the area. It offers a wide range of shops, restaurants, and entertainment options.

What to Buy

- **Department Stores**: Garbera features major department stores where you can find clothing, home goods, and more.
- **Specialty Shops**: The mall includes specialty shops for sports equipment, toys, and gifts.
- **Entertainment**: The shopping centre also has a cinema and play areas for children, making it a family-friendly destination.

Shopping Tips

- **Transport**: Garbera is easily accessible by car and public transport. The mall offers ample parking and regular bus services from the city center.

- **Events**: Check the mall's event calendar for special promotions, workshops, and entertainment activities.

Souvenirs and Artisan Goods

Overview

San Sebastian offers a variety of unique souvenirs and artisan goods that make perfect gifts or keepsakes. From traditional Basque crafts to gourmet food items, there's something for everyone.

Top Souvenir Shops

Basque Store

Overview

The Basque Store, located in the Old Town, offers a curated selection of Basque-themed gifts and souvenirs. It's a great place to find unique items that celebrate Basque culture.

What to Buy

- **Basque Linens**: Look for traditional Basque linens, including tablecloths, napkins, and aprons, featuring vibrant patterns and colors.

- **Local Crafts**: The store offers a range of handcrafted items, from pottery to wooden toys.

- **Books and Music**: Find books on Basque culture and history, as well as CDs of traditional Basque music.

Karrikarte

Overview

Karrikarte, located in the Gros neighborhood, is a charming shop specializing in artisan crafts and local products. It's a great place to discover unique, handmade items.

What to Buy

- **Ceramics**: The store features beautifully crafted ceramics, including plates, bowls, and decorative pieces.
- **Textiles**: Find a variety of textiles, from handwoven blankets to embroidered cushions.
- **Jewelry**: Karrikarte offers a selection of artisan jewelry, each piece reflecting the craftsmanship and creativity of local artists.

La Tetería

Overview

For tea lovers, La Tetería in the city center is a must-visit. This quaint shop offers a wide variety of teas and tea-related products, making it a unique place to find a special gift.

What to Buy

- **Tea Blends**: The shop offers an extensive selection of loose-leaf teas, including traditional blends and unique flavors.

- **Teapots and Accessories**: Find beautifully designed teapots, cups, and other tea accessories.

- **Gourmet Treats**: The store also stocks gourmet treats like biscuits and chocolates that pair perfectly with a cup of tea.

Artisan Markets

San Sebastian hosts several artisan markets throughout the year, where you can find unique handmade items directly from local artists and craftspeople.

Mercado de la Bretxa Artisan Market

Held regularly at La Bretxa Market, this artisan market features stalls selling a variety of handmade goods, from jewelry to clothing to home decor.

What to Buy

- **Handmade Jewelry**: Look for unique, handcrafted pieces that make great souvenirs or gifts.

- **Textiles and Clothing**: Find beautifully made scarves, shawls, and other clothing items.

- **Art and Prints**: Discover original artwork and prints by local artists, perfect for adding a touch of Basque culture to your home.

Shopping Tips

- **Timing**: Artisan markets are typically held on weekends and during special events, so check the local calendar for dates.

- **Cash**: Many vendors may prefer cash, so be sure to have some on hand for your purchases.

San Sebastian offers a rich and diverse shopping experience that reflects its unique blend of traditional Basque culture and modern sophistication. Whether you're exploring bustling local markets, browsing unique boutique stores, shopping at contemporary malls, or hunting for special souvenirs and artisan goods, there's something for every shopper. The city's vibrant shopping scene is a testament to its cultural richness and commitment to quality, making San Sebastian a must-visit destination for anyone who loves to shop. Whether you're looking for high-end fashion, gourmet foods, or unique handmade items, you're sure to find treasures that will remind you of your visit to this beautiful coastal city.

Day Trips from San Sebastian

San Sebastian is not only a beautiful and vibrant city but also a perfect base for exploring the stunning Basque Country and beyond. Here are four fantastic day trips you can take from San Sebastian to experience more of the region's rich culture, history, and natural beauty: Getaria, Hondarribia, Zarautz, and Biarritz (France).

Getaria

Overview

Getaria is a charming fishing village located about 25 kilometers west of San Sebastian. Known for its picturesque harbor, historic sites, and delicious seafood, Getaria is a perfect destination for a relaxing day trip.

Attractions

Cristobal Balenciaga Museum

Dedicated to the legendary fashion designer Cristobal Balenciaga, who was born in Getaria, this museum showcases his life and work. The museum's extensive collection includes some of Balenciaga's most iconic creations, providing a fascinating insight into the history of fashion.

Getaria Lighthouse

Situated on Mount San Antón, also known as the "Mouse of Getaria" due to its distinctive shape, the

Getaria Lighthouse offers stunning views of the coastline. The walk up to the lighthouse is scenic, with lush vegetation and panoramic vistas.

Church of San Salvador

This Gothic-style church, built in the 14th century, is one of Getaria's most significant historical landmarks. Its impressive architecture and beautiful interior make it worth a visit.

Activities

Wine Tasting

Getaria is located in the heart of the Txakoli wine region, known for its crisp, slightly sparkling white wine. Visit a local winery, such as Txakoli Elkano or Bodega Ameztoi, for a tour and tasting session.

Beaches

Getaria has two lovely beaches, Gaztetape and Malkorbe, perfect for sunbathing, swimming, and surfing. The clear waters and golden sands make for a relaxing beach day.

Dining

Getaria is famous for its seafood, particularly grilled fish. Restaurants like Elkano and Kaia-Kaipe are renowned for their fresh, locally caught fish and traditional Basque dishes.

Hondarribia

Overview

Hondarribia is a picturesque coastal town located about 20 kilometers east of San Sebastian, near the French border. With its well-preserved medieval architecture, charming old town, and vibrant marina, Hondarribia is a delightful day trip destination.

Attractions

Old Town (Casco Viejo)

The old town of Hondarribia is a maze of narrow, cobblestone streets lined with colorful houses adorned with

flower-filled balconies. Highlights include:

- **Plaza de Armas**: This central square is surrounded by historic buildings, including the Parador de Hondarribia, a converted 10th-century castle that now serves as a luxury hotel.

- **Church of Santa María de la Asunción y del Manzano**: This Gothic-Renaissance church features beautiful stained glass windows and a striking altarpiece.

- **City Walls and Gates**: The well-preserved city walls and gates, such as the Puerta de Santa María, offer a glimpse into the town's medieval past.

Marina and Waterfront

The marina area is lively, with numerous cafes, bars, and restaurants overlooking the water. It's a great place to enjoy a leisurely meal or a drink while watching the boats.

Activities

Boat Trips

Take a short boat trip across the Bidasoa River to Hendaye, France. The ferry ride offers stunning views of both the Spanish and French coastlines.

Beach

Hondarribia's beach, located near the marina, is a lovely spot for swimming, sunbathing, and beach volleyball. The calm waters make it ideal for families.

Dining

Hondarribia is known for its pintxos bars, particularly in the Marina district. Popular spots include Gran Sol and Sardara, where you can enjoy creative pintxos made with fresh, local ingredients.

Zarautz

Overview

Zarautz is a vibrant seaside town located about 20 kilometers west of San Sebastian. Known for its long sandy beach, excellent surfing conditions, and lively atmosphere, Zarautz is a favorite destination for both locals and tourists.

Attractions

Zarautz Beach

Zarautz boasts the longest beach in the Basque Country, stretching over 2.5 kilometers. It's a popular spot for surfers, swimmers, and sunbathers. The beach is well-equipped with facilities, including showers, restrooms, and beach bars.

Talai Berri Winery

Located on the outskirts of Zarautz, Talai Berri Winery offers tours and tastings of Txakoli wine.

Learn about the wine-making process and enjoy stunning views of the vineyards and the sea.

Activities

Surfing

Zarautz is renowned for its excellent surfing conditions. Surf schools such as Pukas Surf Eskola offer lessons for all levels, making it a great place to catch some waves.

Hiking

The coastal hike from Zarautz to Getaria offers breathtaking views of the sea and cliffs. The well-marked path, part of the Camino de Santiago, takes you through vineyards and offers numerous photo opportunities.

Dining

Zarautz has a vibrant dining scene, with many restaurants offering fresh seafood and traditional Basque cuisine. Restaurante Karlos Arguiñano, located right on the beach, is famous for its delicious dishes and stunning views.

Biarritz (France)

Overview

Located about 50 kilometers from San Sebastian, Biarritz is a chic seaside town on the French Basque coast. Known for its beautiful beaches, elegant architecture, and vibrant cultural scene, Biarritz offers a taste of French sophistication with a Basque twist.

Attractions

Grande Plage

Grande Plage is Biarritz's main beach, known for its golden sands and clear waters. It's a popular spot for sunbathing, swimming, and surfing. The beach is flanked by the iconic Hotel du Palais and numerous cafes and restaurants.

Rocher de la Vierge

This dramatic rock formation, topped with a statue of the Virgin Mary, offers stunning views of the Bay of Biscay. A footbridge connects the rock to the mainland, making it accessible for visitors.

Biarritz Aquarium

The Biarritz Aquarium, also known as the Musée de la Mer, is a fascinating attraction featuring marine life from the Bay of Biscay and beyond. The aquarium's highlights include a large shark tank and a sea lion enclosure.

Activities

Surfing

Biarritz is considered one of Europe's top surfing destinations. The beaches of Côte des Basques and Grande Plage are particularly popular with surfers. Surf schools and rental shops are plentiful, making it easy to get started.

Thalassotherapy

Biarritz is famous for its thalassotherapy centers, which offer treatments using seawater and marine products. A visit to one of these spas, such as Thalmar or Atlanthal, provides a relaxing and rejuvenating experience.

Dining

Biarritz offers a range of dining options, from casual cafes to gourmet restaurants. For a taste of traditional Basque cuisine, try a meal at Chez Albert, known for its seafood dishes. For a more upscale experience, visit L'Atelier, which offers modern French cuisine in an elegant setting.

Day trips from San Sebastian offer a diverse range of experiences, from exploring charming fishing villages and historic towns to enjoying beautiful beaches and vibrant cultural scenes. Whether you're savoring fresh seafood in Getaria, wandering the medieval streets of Hondarribia, surfing the waves in Zarautz, or experiencing the chic atmosphere of Biarritz, each destination provides its own unique glimpse into the rich tapestry of the Basque Country and beyond. These day trips not only enhance your visit to San Sebastian but also create lasting memories of the region's incredible beauty and cultural richness.

Practical Information

When visiting San Sebastian, having practical information at your fingertips can ensure a smooth and enjoyable trip. Here's a detailed guide covering emergency contacts, health and safety tips, language and communication, money and banking, and internet and mobile connectivity.

Emergency Contacts

In case of emergencies, knowing the right contacts is crucial. San Sebastian, like the rest of Spain, has a robust system for handling emergencies efficiently.

General Emergency Number: 112

Dial 112 for any type of emergency, including medical, fire, or police. This is a Europe-wide emergency number and operators can typically assist in multiple languages, including English.

Police: 091

For police assistance, you can also dial 091. This number connects you to the National Police, who handle general law enforcement duties.

Local Police: 092

For non-urgent police matters within San Sebastian, dial 092 to reach the local municipal police (Policía Municipal). They handle local incidents, traffic issues, and community safety.

Medical Emergencies: 061

For urgent medical assistance, you can call 061 to connect with emergency medical services. Operators will dispatch an ambulance if necessary.

Nearest Hospital

The main hospital in San Sebastian is Hospital Universitario Donostia, located at Paseo Dr. Begiristain, s/n. It is well-equipped and provides comprehensive medical services.

Health and Safety Tips

Health Tips

- **Pharmacies**: Pharmacies (farmacias) are abundant in San Sebastian and easily recognizable by a green cross. They can provide over-the-counter medications and basic health advice. Many pharmacies have 24-hour service on a rotating basis.

- **Travel Insurance**: It's advisable to have travel insurance that covers health care. EU citizens can use their European Health Insurance Card (EHIC) for emergency medical treatment.

- **Vaccinations**: No special vaccinations are required for travel to Spain, but it's good to ensure routine vaccinations are up to date.

Safety Tips

- **Personal Belongings**: Like any tourist destination, be mindful of your belongings to avoid pickpocketing. Keep your valuables secure and be especially cautious in crowded areas.

- **Local Laws**: Familiarize yourself with local laws and customs. For example, drinking alcohol in public spaces outside designated areas is generally prohibited.

- **Emergency Services**: Save emergency numbers on your phone and know the location of the nearest hospital and police station.

Language and Communication

Language

The official languages in San Sebastian are Spanish (Castellano) and Basque (Euskara). While Spanish is widely spoken, Basque is an important cultural element and you will see it on signs and hear it spoken by locals.

Communication Tips

- **Basic Phrases**: Learning a few basic phrases in Spanish or Basque can be very helpful. Phrases like "hola" (hello), "gracias" (thank you), and "por favor" (please) in Spanish, or "kaixo" (hello), "eskerrik asko" (thank you), and "mesedez" (please) in Basque, are appreciated.

- **Language Apps**: Consider using language translation apps or carrying a phrasebook to assist with communication.

- **English Speakers**: Many people in the tourism industry, such as hotel staff and restaurant workers, speak English. However, it's beneficial to try using Spanish or Basque, especially in more local settings.

Money and Banking

Currency

The currency in San Sebastian is the Euro (€). It's advisable to have some cash on hand for small purchases, though credit and debit cards are widely accepted.

ATMs

ATMs are plentiful throughout the city, and most accept international cards. Look for ATMs at banks, in shopping areas, and near tourist attractions.

Banks

Major banks in San Sebastian include BBVA, Santander, and CaixaBank. These banks offer a range of services, including currency exchange and international money transfers.

Currency Exchange

Currency exchange services are available at banks, exchange offices (cambios), and some hotels. It's usually better to exchange currency at a bank for better rates.

Tipping

Tipping is not mandatory in Spain but is appreciated for good service. In restaurants, a tip of 5-10% is customary if service was particularly good. For taxis, rounding up to the nearest Euro is common. Small tips for hotel staff and tour guides are also appreciated.

Internet and Mobile Connectivity

Internet Access

- **Wi-Fi**: Free Wi-Fi is widely available in San Sebastian. Many cafes, restaurants, and hotels offer complimentary Wi-Fi to customers. Public places like parks and libraries may also provide free internet access.

- **Internet Cafes**: If you need reliable internet access and don't have a device, internet cafes (locutorios) are available in the city.

Mobile Connectivity

- **SIM Cards**: If you're planning to stay for an extended period, consider purchasing a local SIM card. Providers like Movistar, Vodafone, and Orange offer prepaid SIM cards with data plans. These are available at mobile phone stores and some convenience stores.

- **Roaming**: EU residents can use their mobile phones in Spain without incurring additional roaming charges. For non-EU residents, check with your provider about international roaming plans.

- **Coverage**: Mobile network coverage in San Sebastian is generally excellent, with strong signal strength throughout the city and surrounding areas.

Apps to Download

- **Transportation Apps**: Apps like Google Maps, Moovit, and Dbus (local bus service) are useful for navigating the city.

- **Language Apps**: Duolingo, Google Translate, and other language apps can assist with communication.

- **Travel Apps**: TripAdvisor, Yelp, and similar apps can help you find top-rated restaurants, attractions, and services in San Sebastian.

Armed with practical information, you're well-prepared to enjoy your visit to San Sebastian. From knowing how to handle emergencies and staying safe and healthy, to navigating language barriers and managing money and banking, these tips will help ensure a smooth and enjoyable experience. With its rich cultural heritage, stunning scenery, and vibrant lifestyle, San Sebastian is a city that promises a memorable stay. Whether you're exploring local markets, indulging in the culinary scene, or simply soaking up the Basque charm, being well-informed will enhance your adventure in this beautiful coastal city.

Travel Tips

Planning a trip to San Sebastian requires some thoughtful preparation to ensure you make the most of your visit. Here are some essential travel tips, including the best time to visit, cultural etiquette, packing essentials, and accessibility information.

Best Time to Visit

Spring (March to May)

Spring is an excellent time to visit San Sebastian. The weather is mild, with temperatures ranging from 10°C (50°F) to 20°C (68°F). The city is less crowded than in the summer, making it a pleasant time for sightseeing and outdoor activities.

- **Pros**: Mild weather, fewer tourists, beautiful blooming landscapes.
- **Cons**: Some attractions and restaurants may have limited hours.

Summer (June to August)

Summer is the peak tourist season in San Sebastian, with warm weather and plenty of sunshine. Temperatures typically range from 20°C (68°F) to 28°C (82°F). This is the best time to enjoy the beaches and outdoor festivals.

- **Pros**: Ideal beach weather, numerous festivals and events, lively atmosphere.
- **Cons**: Crowded, higher accommodation prices.

Autumn (September to November)

Autumn is another great time to visit San Sebastian. The weather remains pleasant, with temperatures ranging from 15°C (59°F) to 25°C (77°F). The crowds thin out after the summer, and the city hosts several notable events.

- **Pros**: Mild weather, fewer crowds, San Sebastian International Film Festival.
- **Cons**: Unpredictable weather, shorter daylight hours.

Winter (December to February)

Winter is the off-season in San Sebastian, with cooler temperatures ranging from 8°C (46°F) to 14°C (57°F). While it's not beach weather, the city's charm remains, and it's a great time to experience the local culture without the crowds.

- **Pros**: Fewer tourists, lower prices, festive holiday atmosphere.
- **Cons**: Cooler weather, some attractions may be closed.

Cultural Etiquette

Greetings

In San Sebastian, greetings are usually warm and friendly. It's common to greet people with a handshake or, among friends and family, with a kiss on each cheek.

- **Useful Phrases**: "Hola" (hello), "Buenos días" (good morning), "Buenas tardes" (good afternoon/evening).

Dining

When dining out, it's customary to greet the staff upon entering and thank them when leaving. Spaniards typically have lunch around 2 PM and dinner around 9 PM. It's polite to wait until everyone is served before starting your meal.

- **Tipping**: Tipping is appreciated but not mandatory. Leaving a 5-10% tip for good service is common.

Dress Code

San Sebastian is relatively casual, but it's good to dress smartly, especially when dining out or attending events. Beachwear is appropriate at the beach, but cover up when leaving the beach area.

Public Behavior

Spaniards are generally open and expressive, but it's important to respect local customs and traditions. Avoid loud or disruptive behavior in public places, and always be respectful in religious and historical sites.

Packing Essentials

Clothing

- **Layered Clothing**: The weather can vary, so pack layers that you can add or remove as needed. Lightweight clothes for summer and warmer layers for cooler seasons are recommended.

- **Comfortable Shoes**: San Sebastian's cobblestone streets and hilly terrain make comfortable walking shoes essential.

- **Beachwear**: If visiting in summer, bring swimwear, a beach towel, and sun protection.

- **Rain Gear**: A light raincoat or umbrella is useful, especially in the spring and autumn.

Travel Accessories

- **Daypack**: A small backpack for daily excursions and carrying essentials.

- **Water Bottle**: Stay hydrated while exploring the city.

- **Travel Guide and Maps**: While digital maps are convenient, a physical guidebook and maps can be handy.

Health and Safety

- **Medications**: Bring any necessary medications, along with copies of your prescriptions.

- **First Aid Kit**: Include basics like band-aids, antiseptic wipes, and pain relievers.

- **Sun Protection**: Sunscreen, sunglasses, and a hat are essential for summer visits.

Electronics

- **Universal Adapter**: Spain uses Type C and F plugs, so bring a universal adapter for your devices.

- **Portable Charger**: Keep your phone and camera charged while on the go.
- **Camera**: Capture the beautiful scenery and memorable moments.

Accessibility Information

General Accessibility

San Sebastian is relatively accessible, with many hotels, restaurants, and attractions equipped to accommodate visitors with mobility challenges. The city is making continuous efforts to improve accessibility.

Transportation

- **Buses**: The city's bus network is equipped with low-floor buses and ramps, making public transportation accessible.
- **Taxis**: Accessible taxis are available, but it's advisable to book in advance.

- **Train Stations**: The main train stations, including Donostia-San Sebastián station, have facilities for disabled passengers.

Attractions

Many of San Sebastian's main attractions, such as La Concha Beach and the San Telmo Museum, are accessible. However, some historical sites and older buildings may have limited access.

- **Beaches**: La Concha Beach has accessible ramps and pathways for wheelchair users.
- **Museums**: Major museums like San Telmo Museum and the Aquarium have accessible entrances and facilities.

Accommodation

When booking accommodation, check for accessibility features such as elevators, ramps, and accessible bathrooms. Many hotels and guesthouses in San Sebastian offer accessible rooms and services.

Assistance Services

- **Tourist Information**: The San Sebastian Tourism Office provides information on accessible routes and services in the city.

- **Medical Services**: The city has excellent healthcare facilities, and many pharmacies are equipped to assist with medical needs.

Planning a trip to San Sebastian involves more than just choosing the right attractions. By considering the best time to visit, understanding local cultural etiquette, packing appropriately, and knowing about accessibility options, you can ensure a smooth and enjoyable experience. San Sebastian's welcoming atmosphere, combined with its stunning scenery and rich cultural heritage, makes it a fantastic destination for all travelers.

Conclusion

Final Thoughts

San Sebastian, or Donostia as it is known in Basque, is a city that effortlessly combines natural beauty, rich culture, and culinary excellence. Whether you are drawn to its stunning beaches, vibrant festivals, historic landmarks, or world-renowned cuisine, San Sebastian promises an unforgettable experience. The city's charm lies in its ability to offer something for every type of traveler, from the food enthusiast to the history buff, the beach lover to the adventure seeker.

Cultural Richness

San Sebastian is steeped in Basque culture and tradition. Visitors can explore the rich history and unique identity of the Basque people through the city's museums, festivals, and daily life. The San

Telmo Museum, for instance, provides a comprehensive look at Basque history, while the city's numerous festivals, such as the San Sebastian International Film Festival and Semana Grande, offer immersive cultural experiences.

Culinary Excellence

Known as one of the world's top culinary destinations, San Sebastian boasts a food scene that is both innovative and deeply rooted in tradition. The city's pintxos bars are legendary, offering a tapas experience that is unique to the Basque Country. For those seeking high-end dining, San Sebastian is home to several Michelin-starred restaurants, including the famed Arzak, Akelarre, and Mugaritz, each offering exquisite menus that showcase the best of Basque cuisine.

Natural Beauty

The city's natural beauty is undeniable, with its golden beaches, lush green hills, and picturesque bay. La Concha Beach, often cited as one of the most beautiful urban beaches in the world, provides a perfect setting for relaxation and water activities. The surrounding hills, such as Monte Urgull and Monte Igueldo, offer stunning views and hiking opportunities for those looking to explore the natural landscape.

Accessibility and Convenience

San Sebastian is well-connected and easy to navigate, making it a convenient destination for travelers. The city's public transportation system is efficient, and its compact size means that many attractions are within walking distance. Additionally, San Sebastian's commitment to accessibility ensures that all visitors, including those with mobility challenges, can enjoy what the city has to offer.

San Sebastian is a city that captures the heart and soul of its visitors. Whether you come for its food, culture, natural beauty, or simply to relax and enjoy the Basque way of life, you will leave with unforgettable memories and a desire to return.

FAQs

What is the best time to visit San Sebastian?

The best time to visit San Sebastian depends on your preferences. Summer (June to August) is ideal for beach activities and festivals, but it is also the busiest time. Spring (March to May) and autumn (September to November) offer mild weather and fewer crowds, making them great times for sightseeing and outdoor activities. Winter (December to February) is the off-season, with cooler weather but a charming holiday atmosphere.

How do I get to San Sebastian?

San Sebastian is accessible by air, train, bus, and car. The nearest airports are San Sebastian Airport (EAS), Bilbao Airport (BIO), and Biarritz Airport (BIQ) in France. The city is well-connected by train, with services from major Spanish cities and nearby France. Buses also run frequently from various locations. If you are driving, the city is easily reachable via well-maintained highways.

What are some must-try foods in San Sebastian?

When in San Sebastian, don't miss trying pintxos, the Basque version of tapas. Popular pintxos include "gilda" (a skewer of olives, anchovies, and pickled peppers), "txangurro" (stuffed crab), and "bacalao" (salted cod). Additionally, try traditional Basque dishes such as "marmitako" (tuna and potato stew) and "chuletón" (Basque-style grilled steak). For dessert, "pantxineta" (a pastry filled with custard) is a local favorite.

Is San Sebastian a good destination for families?

Yes, San Sebastian is an excellent destination for families. The city offers a variety of family-friendly activities, including beaches with safe swimming areas, parks, and attractions such as the San

Sebastian Aquarium and the Monte Igueldo amusement park. Many restaurants and hotels also cater to families, providing amenities and services to ensure a comfortable stay.

What are some popular day trips from San Sebastian?

Popular day trips from San Sebastian include visits to nearby towns and attractions such as Getaria, Hondarribia, Zarautz, and Biarritz (France). Each destination offers unique experiences, from historic sites and beautiful beaches to charming villages and vibrant markets.

What is the local language, and will I need to speak Spanish or Basque?

The official languages in San Sebastian are Spanish and Basque. While knowing some basic Spanish phrases can be helpful, especially in more local settings, many people in the tourism industry speak English. Learning a few Basque phrases can also enhance your cultural experience and is appreciated by locals.

How safe is San Sebastian for tourists?

San Sebastian is generally considered a safe city for tourists. However, as with any destination, it's important to take common-sense precautions, such as keeping an eye on your belongings, especially in crowded areas, and avoiding poorly lit or isolated areas at night. Emergency services are reliable, and the city is well-policed.

What should I pack for a trip to San Sebastian?

What you pack depends on the time of year you visit. In general, bring comfortable walking shoes, layered clothing, beachwear (if visiting in summer), a raincoat or umbrella, and sun protection. Don't forget essential travel documents, medications, and a universal power adapter for your electronics.

Are there any local customs or etiquette I should be aware of?

When dining out, it's polite to greet the staff upon entering and thank them when leaving. Spaniards typically have lunch around 2 PM and dinner around 9 PM. It's also customary to wait until everyone is served before starting your meal. Dress smartly when dining out or attending events, and always be respectful in religious and historical sites.

San Sebastian is a city that leaves a lasting impression on its visitors. Armed with these travel tips and insights, you're well-prepared to enjoy all that this beautiful Basque city has to offer. Whether you're exploring its cultural landmarks, indulging in its culinary delights, or simply soaking up its scenic beauty, San Sebastian promises an unforgettable experience.

Printed in Great Britain
by Amazon